BASED ON A

A Cord of THREE STRANDS

A Story of God's Woven Grace

SARA W. BERRY AND TRICIA J. ROBBINS

Tupelo, Mississippi

ISBN: 978-0-9845426-1-1
Printed in the United States of America

Cover Design and Interior Layout Design:
Tracy Applewhite Broome
www.tracybroome.com

Special thanks to Ellie Berry for help with the Interior Layout Design

Cover photography:
Patrick Wright
www.ppgportraits.co

Editorial Assistance:
Beth Clark, Nashville, TN

Author photography for Sara Berry:
Stephanie Rhea
www.stephanierhea.net

Author photography for Tricia Robbins and Interior Layout Photography:
Jennifer Crook
www.jennifercrookphotography.com

Bethel Road Publications, Tupelo, MS
www.bethelroadpublications.com

What People Are Saying ....

"As one reads this engaging story, it is difficult sometimes to remember that it's true. Berry and Robbins' story-telling skills, as well as the story itself, perfectly reflect the three-strand metaphor as they artfully weave together the three stories. It is an emotional story to read, but it is fully satisfying because it tells the story of God's grace and redemptive power even when our worst nature makes us try to run from Him. But He is faithful. Powerful. Strong. Loving. He is a God of hope. And He is able to bring us to Himself. That's the God so beautifully represented in ***A Cord of Three Strands*** and in the lives of the story's three strong women."

Randall Murphree, Editor
American Family Association Journal magazine

"***A Cord of Three Strands*** is the best book I have ever read. It is inspiring as a Christian and as a teen to see how God has plans for our lives that are bigger than we could ever imagine."

Chloe, Mississippi
High School student

"Finished the book last night! AWESOME! Glory to God! Such a gift to be reminded of His redeeming love."

Kelli, Tennessee

"Based on a true story, three women grapple with hurts, baggage, rebellion and unfulfilled dreams. Their lives intersect in a way only God could orchestrate ... God's grace is everywhere in this story."

Marilyn H. Tinnin, Publisher
and Editor of Metro Christian Living Magazine

"Powerful testimony of God's redeeming love, grace and mercy. Only

God could have woven this story. I recommend the book for anyone, women and men, who has ever found themselves questioning, 'God are you there?' This book proves He is there and listening and answering in His own perfect way and His own perfect time."

Tony, Mississippi

"I read it in one sitting, from the airport to the plane and all the way to Denver. Of course there were a couple of tears and the lady next to me might have thought I was crazy, but it was so beautiful and I loved it."

Adriene, Colorado

"I just started and finished the book in three hours! This was such an incredible testament to His love for us!"

Cristell, Washington

"Wow, what an awesome book! It is an inspiring book of God's grace, mercy and redemption. The book grabbed me from the beginning and I could not put it down. I stayed up until 2:00 a.m. one morning to finish it. I feel this book will be a great tool in the kingdom of God. An incredible story that demonstrates what the devil intended for evil, God turned it around for good. I would recommend this book for both men and women. To God be the Glory -- great things He has done!!"

Maxine, Florida

"Just finished the book last night! AMAZING story! Loved every single page. Thank you!!! Will recommend to everyone."

Leah, Mississippi

"I was so enthralled by the story... read the whole book that night! Blown away!!"

Kyra, Alabama

"My mom brought me the book last week and I LOVED reading the story!!! To God be the glory!! I will be passing it around to my English speaking friends here!!"

Whitney, Peru

"I just wanted to personally tell you how much I enjoyed ***A Cord of Three Strands***. I picked it up this morning for the first time and COULD NOT put it down! What an amazing story! If anybody wants a good book to read, I HIGHLY recommend this book! Thanks for sharing this story."

Allison, Mississippi

"Wow! I just read your book and was moved so many times to tears. Just simply could not put it down. What a beautiful story God delivered... I just feel like I know the people in the book personally! As God always does, He repeated many scriptures to me personally that I have been reading over lately. Praise God!"

Marcy, Tennessee

"I just finished ***A Cord of Three Strands*** and to say it was FABULOUS would be an understatement! I finished it in two sittings and cried ALL the way through it! What a wonderful work it is! Thank you for bringing that story to light!"

Karen, Mississippi

"I finished reluctantly... wanting the book to go on and on! Was a beautiful illustration of God's sovereignty, grace and love!"

Julie, Mississippi

"I just finished ***A Cord of Three Strands*** and wanted to tell you how much I enjoyed the book!! What a great story! In my opinion every teenage girl should read it... it was a joy to read!"

Valerie, Mississippi

Acknowledgments

Sara W. Berry

I remember the day I went to lunch with Tricia for the first time. Normally, new friends don't spend three hours sharing their life stories with each other. But this is not a normal friend! I praise God for Tricia and her willingness to share her story with the world. It has been my great honor to be a part of that.

Hilarie and Peggy, you both have been a joy to work with and I am inspired by your stories and your lives. God has only just begun to use you in mighty ways!

I want to say a deep, heartfelt thank-you to my husband, Mont. He supports me endlessly and is my biggest encourager. He is the love of my life and my best friend. I love you, Mont!

To my six incredible children: Katie, Ellie, Joseph, Troy, Joshua, and Sara Ruth. I marvel at who each of you is becoming. I am so greatly blessed to be your mom. Thanks for letting me write and thanks for your love and encouragement. I couldn't do this otherwise. A special note to Sara Ruth, our own precious adoption story: You have blessed all of our lives beyond measure and have made us more aware of our Father's heart.

Thanks to my mom, Nancy Ann Williams, who told me that we had to go ahead and get this book out there. And thanks to my dad, Kenneth Williams, marathoner extraordinaire, who helped a non-runner describe an accurate runner's experience.

To Kerry, Anna, and Lane, my dear friends and co-workers: I could never finish a project without your help, encouragement, prayers, and editing skills. Thank you from the bottom of my heart.

To Beth Clark, our talented and patient editor: Thanks for helping us take this book to the next level.

To the board and staff of Parkgate Pregnancy Clinic: It is my great honor to serve with you. You each inspire me to serve Him wholeheartedly.

Above all, to my Jesus: You are everything to me! May You receive glory and honor in all things. I pray that this book brings You pleasure!

Acknowledgments

Tricia J. Robbins

I want to give praise and love to my precious Father God who in His beautiful, mercy-filled way has loved me through it all! I can't live or breath without Him! He is my everything!

I want to also say a deep love and gratitude to Shane—my best friend, lover and the person who has seen me through thick and thin! I want to say thank you to my beautiful Morgan and Ethan for being the most amazing kids Mommy could ever ask for! I love you two!

In the deepest love and amazing friendship I thank my precious Hilarie—you have blessed me as a best friend and sister and I love doing life together! No one will ever truly know how happy we are to have each other!

Thank you my precious parents who have loved me and walked through everything with me! You both mean the world to me! Thank you to April, Wayne and Wendy—the best friends and siblings I could ever have! I praise God for the closeness between us all.

Thank you to Mitch and Peggy for your love and generous spirit! My love is so deep for you both.

Thank you to the best girlfriends who have walked very closely with me through all of this: Julie, Jennifer, Christian, and Traci. I love you girls!

Thank you to the beautiful Parkgate staff, Jessica, Carrie, Misty, and the board—this place has my heart!

Thank you to Sara for being Spirit filled and Spirit led—you are my dear friend and I respect and appreciate you so much!

Lastly, thank you to my dearest Pat. Thank you for showing me His unconditional love and for guiding me through such a hard time. I'll always be so grateful for who you are to me! I love you, Pat! To God be all the glory!

Dedication

For every young woman who finds herself
trapped in the web of heartache and confusion,
this book is for you.
May you soon experience the truth of God's amazing grace.

For every parent who is wounded and broken
over the rebellion and rejection of a child,
this book is for you.
May you find comfort and wisdom
in the presence of the Perfect Father.

For every would-be parent longing and waiting
for a child to hold and love,
this book is for you.
May you crawl up into the lap of the Sovereign God
and gain new strength and joy in the waiting.

For every individual called
to love and support any of the above,
this book is for you.
May you be richly blessed
for loving Him by caring for others.

A cord of three strands
is not easily broken.

see Ecclesiastes 4:12

Prologue

She felt the warmth of his hand in hers. Attraction dangerously drew both of them together. They walked to the house where the college party roared with music from the band and laughter from the party-goers. Various groups of young people formed clusters along the lawn and throughout the house.

The stairs creaked as they walked together up to the front porch. *I hope this old porch holds all these people,* she thought. The scene was fairly new to her. She had just recently begun hanging with this crowd, introduced to her by the young man at her side. She still didn't feel totally comfortable; she wasn't really a college student yet, but each party brought with it a more familiar experience.

At first, she felt guilty. Her life now was certainly different than it was just a few months before, when she stood dressed in cap and gown with the graduating class of 1990. Throughout high school, this party scene was the kind of situation that her parents had always warned her about.

But they were wrong. These were great people who had welcomed her into their circle of friendship and fun. With each gathering the guilt slipped further and further from her conscience. She liked the way she felt when she was with her new friends—carefree, fun-loving, grown-up, but not the stuffy kind of grown-up. It was the excitement of something new and different. It was the feeling of being a part of a group who never questioned her, just accepted her. It was fun.

The pair entered the house, bumping into people and screaming hello to familiar faces over the loud sound of the drums, electric guitar, and deep bass of the band. Even her taste in music was expanding. She was glad. She had been sheltered too long in the world of doing exactly what was expected of her. Her growing relationship with her Savior had come to a screeching halt. *But surely He understands,* she thought as guilt plagued her late at night, when the parties were over and sleep evaded her. *I do have freedom in Christ. The Bible talks a lot about that. I am just exerting my freedom in Christ,* she tried to convince herself night after night.

In a relatively short amount of time, sleep no longer evaded her. Guilt no longer plagued her. She simply enjoyed this new phase of her life.

The couple continued through the house to the back porch where "confidence in a cup" waited to be dispersed from the keg outside. She sipped hers slowly, still not sure whether she liked it or not, but unwilling to set herself apart by refusing the offer. She parted from him temporarily in order to speak to a new friend, whom she spotted sitting on a torn, floral sofa placed awkwardly in the grass next to the broken fence.

As she neared, a place on the sofa opened up and she sat down beside her friend. She immediately noticed a terrible aroma of beer, pot, and old age, mingled together and rising from the sofa. She ignored the smell and greeted her friend, who looked at her with a crooked smile and glazed eyes.

"Hey! My favorite friend! Want some?" The girl thrust a small, smoldering stub near her face. One sniff and she knew what it was.

"No, thanks," she said nervously.

"Oh, come on. Just try it. It has medicinal purposes, you know." And with that statement, the girl laughed as if she had just said the most clever punch-line in the history of comedy.

"No, I don't think so. But thanks," she replied.

"Okay," the girl said with disappointment.

Not wanting to offend her new friend, she said, "Well, okay, I guess I could try it."

And with that, a new world opened up for Tricia Johnson. Relaxation, fun, acceptance … forgetting troubles, forgetting past and future, simply being in the fog of freedom and fun.

Chapter 1

Tricia sat on the edge of her small twin bed and looked around the dorm room that had just become her home. Big, black garbage bags were scattered around her side of the room. This was in stark contrast to the neat and cheery side belonging to her roommate. Blessedly, her roommate— *was it Susan?*— was gone for the weekend. Tricia and her parents had met her as they brought in the first load of garbage bags. Thankfully, Susan was not there long enough to realize that *all* of Tricia's belongings came to this, her new home, in the ugly, plastic bags. Her parents, Shirley and Lloyd Johnson, had quickly unloaded and left. All three of them were glad the long, painful trip was over. As her parents left, they both tried to hug her goodbye. Tricia stubbornly left her hands at her side and fixed her countenance in a bitter, emotionless stance. They had both pulled back awkwardly and left quickly. So be it.

Tricia looked again at the garbage bags that held her life's belongings. How ironic. Her life was so messed up, so far from being what she had imagined that it would be now, that the bags seemed to scream at her their symbolism. Her life was trash. She was trash.

A single tear trickled down her cheek. She quickly wiped it away. She didn't want to cry any more. She had cried the entire trip from her home in Tennessee to this new school in Florida—all 12 hours of it. Her head ached from the continuous tears. She was done.

She reached into her backpack and retrieved her Walkman. She put in a cassette tape that her friend, Katherine—Kat for short—had made for her the week before. She thought of Kat, and great longing pierced her heart. She wished that she were with Kat right now, enjoying her constant jokes and carefree life. Kat was petite, with short, dark hair and was edgy in both appearance and attitude. She was fun, fiercly loyal, and a faithful friend. How Tricia missed her already!

Tricia put the soft, round earphones tightly in place and cranked up the volume as loudly as she could stand. The heavy metal sound was in sharp contrast to the type of music that she had preferred over the years. She lay back on the still unmade bed and stared up at the ceiling. A water stain had formed a circle directly over her bed. *Oh, great. I'm sure I will have to deal with the constant drip whenever it storms. Just like Chinese water torture. As if just being here is not torture enough.*

Tired of seeing the water stain, tired of thinking of the future, tired of thinking of the past, Tricia rolled to her side. Her mattress was stained and striped and covered in plastic. The stripes reminded her of jail. Vertical stripes on the mattress, vertical stripes on jail clothes, vertical stripes of the bars of a cell. Though she had never actually been in a jail cell, she felt she was in prison. The bars were the result of her own attitudes and actions. What was she going to do?

Nothing right now. She was just going to continue to lie on the dirty, striped mattress, and let the music drown out any sadness she felt. She curled into a fetal position, and despite her resolve, the tears flowed again.

Chapter 2

Tricia awoke with a start. She wiped the drool from her cheek and took the earphones off her head. Her left ear ached from the pressure of lying on the earphone. *Where am I?* She rolled over and looked around. Rapid memories from the past 24 hours flashed across her mind, like a slide show: Leaving Knoxville, with a carload of garbage bags. Seeing the sun rise just as the Tennessee hills vanished from the scene. Hours of tears and angry words and bitter silence. Twelve hours later, the hot Florida sun setting as she sullenly unloaded bag after bag. She sat up quickly, causing her head to swim. With a new focus of letting the dizziness settle, the slide show of memories faded away.

Across the room she saw pink and blue and yellow and green. Big, pink flowers covered the other twin bed in the room. Wide, polka-dotted, grosgrain ribbon fell in long strips on the wall beside the bright bed. Painted clothes-pins attached happy photos all along the ribbon. Her roommate's smiling face appeared with various people of all ages. A couple, obviously her parents, was proudly hugging their vivacious daughter in several of the photos. And then there were photos of grandparents and friends and siblings.

Oh, joy. I am stuck with Pollyanna for a whole year. I probably don't have a single family photo in all of those garbage bags. And why would I? she thought, *Why would I want to remember home or family?*

Of course, it had not always been this way. In fact, she wasn't really sure how she got to this place of bitterness and heartache. A memory, so sweet it brought tears to her eyes, quickly surfaced to the forefront of her mind.

Tricia, a sweet and innocent fourteen-year-old, played the piano on her parents' baby grand. Her slender, athletic build, light brown hair and green eyes were eye-catching, drawing attention from many. Gone was the little girl. Her five-foot, six inches were womanly and radiant now. She exuded rare, natural beauty that was enviable, and her personality was marked by energy, creativity, and passion for life. Her parents marveled at the talented and beautiful young woman she was becoming. Indeed, they were blessed.

Tricia's fingers flew over the keys with both strength and gentleness. The notes of the classical piece were soothing and inspiring. She finished the piece with the perfection she was known for. As she looked up, she saw her mother standing in the doorway, leaning against the doorframe. She held her hands loosely together in front of her. Her face was peaceful and relaxed. The slight smile on her face showed the love and pride and gratefulness that she felt at that moment. Her beautiful, talented Tricia filled her with such joy. How could one person be so full of life and light and love? Yes, mother and daughter were very different. Tricia always pushed. Tricia was energetic and funny and talented. And thankfully, Tricia loved Jesus. She had prayed with her to receive Christ when she was just seven years old. *And it's a good thing,* her mom thought. *There is a bit of a discontent in her personality that, untamed, could lead to rebellion. Yes, it is a good thing that Tricia surrendered to the Lord at a young age.*

Tricia, looked up and smiled at her mom. "Ready for bed?" she asked her mom.

"Yes, honey, and you shouldn't be too far behind me."

"Yes, Ma'am," she replied reluctantly. "But first, do you have any requests tonight?" she asked.

Her mom replied, "How about *Amazing Grace*?"

"Sounds good. Night, Mom."

"Good night, Tricia. I love you."

"Love you too."

As her mom headed toward her bedroom, Tricia began to play the familiar tune. The words of the song, unspoken, played in her mind as her fingers flowed over the keys. Soon she was lost in the music and lost in the unspoken words.

Amazing Grace! How sweet the sound!
That saved a wretch like me.
I once was lost, but now am found!
Was blind but now I see!

She played through every verse of the song, silently singing along. And then, as often was the case, her fingers began to add to the song a new melody with new notes, even unknown to Tricia. This was her act of worship. This was her gift to her Savior and to her family. She played for a long time, lost in the music, as the beautiful notes lulled her family to sleep. This was their nightly routine. None could have imagined the changes to come.

ooooooo

Back in the present, Tricia sat up on her still unmade bed. The sweet memory created a longing deep in the pit of her stomach. *If only I could go back. How had things changed so quickly? If only…*

Another memory surfaced to the forefront of her mind. This one had the same setting, but a much different tone. This memory was more recent, and unfortunately, had been repeated with much the same dialog too many times.

Tricia, not so sweet or innocent, played the piano on her parents' baby grand. Her fingers flew over the keys with too much strength. This strength of motion was fueled by frustration and discontent and anger. Yes, anger was probably the strongest emotion. No *Amazing Grace* tonight. Tonight she sought through music to deal with the negative emotions she was becoming all too familiar with. She pounded the keys. The notes, though played with excellence, could not be considered beautiful—at least not to anyone in this family.

In the middle of the song, Tricia glanced up to see her mother standing in the doorway. She did not lean into a relaxed position against the doorpost. No, this time she stood mid doorway with arms crossed and angry eyes staring at Tricia. For a brief moment, Tricia saw just a glimpse of something besides anger. What was that look that she saw skim across her mother's eyes so often these days? Worry? Fear?

Well, let her worry! Let her be afraid. She can't control me anymore! Probably that look is more disappointment than anything else, Tricia thought bitterly. *I don't care! Let her be disappointed. I am who I am, and she can't change me.*

Tricia looked up at her mother defiantly. "What?" she asked impatiently.

"Time for bed," her mother replied.

"Well, go ahead. I'm not stopping you."

"No, Tricia, I mean it is time for *you* to go to bed."

"I always play at night. You always let me play while you go to sleep."

"That's not the kind of music anyone can go to sleep to."

"So, you are saying you don't like my music?"

"No, Tricia, I am saying it is time for bed. Now."

"Fine!" Tricia loudly and dramatically pushed the piano stool back, scraping the wooden floor in the process. Her mother's eyes seethed, but she said nothing. She simply stood, with arms still crossed, and glared.

Tricia stomped up the stairs. Both mother and daughter went to bed very angry. But this was nothing new.

Chapter 3

Peggy McGill drank the last sip of her second cup of coffee as she rose slowly from the kitchen table. Her petite stature and medium frame was usually fueled by optimism and energy. But today, she just felt weary.

Time to get going. No need to prolong it any more. She and her husband, Mitch, had another appointment with the adoption agency. One would think she would be excited, overjoyed even. But instead, she felt cautious and fragile. *Surely, something will work out soon,* she thought. She rinsed her coffee cup and put it in the dishwasher, and then ran water from the faucet over a paper towel. She then wiped the same spot on the counter over and over, as she was deep in thought. Once again, she was tempted to say, "Why, Lord?" She wasn't afraid to say those words. Her relationship with her Lord was so intimate, so sweet, she knew that she would not offend Him. *Jesus asked why, too, when He was hanging on the cross, didn't He?* she thought.

But today, she just felt too tired to ask why. Eighteen

years is a long time to ask, a long time to wonder, a long time to trust. Eighteen years. *Wow,* she thought. *If I had had a baby when I wanted to, he or she would be graduated from high school by now.*

Another thought surfaced. This one seemed to enter her mind more often in the past year or so. *Maybe I am too old to become a mom.* This unpleasant thought brought doubt with it. But Peggy quickly dismissed it. *No, this is my heart's desire. I have surrendered it to the Lord over and over and it has never gone away. I will keep trying until the Lord says to stop. But, Jesus, please protect my heart. I don't know if Mitch and I can take much more disappointment.*

Peggy quickly finished wiping the counters as she shook off her melancholy thoughts. Instead, she fought the depression the only way she knew how—with the sword of the Spirit, the Word of God. As she quickly finished tidying the kitchen, making their bed, and getting dressed, she used this mighty sword, sometimes out loud, sometimes in whispers, sometimes inside her head. But she quoted as many scriptures as she could remember, whether they seemed to apply to this situation or not.

> *No weapon forged against you will prevvail.*
>
> *Isaiah 54:17*

> *For God so loved the world that He gave His one and only Son, that whosoever believes in Him, shall not perish but have eternal life.*
>
> *John 3:16*

No, in all these things we are more than conquerors through him who loved us. For I am convinced that neither death nor life, neither angels nor demons, neither the present nor the future, nor any powers, neither height nor depth, nor anything else in all creation, will be able to separate us from the love of God that is in Christ Jesus our Lord.

Romans 8:37-39

We are destroying speculations and every lofty thing raised up against the knowledge of God, and we are taking every thought captive to the obedience of Christ.

2 Corinthians 10:5, NASB

Be strong and courageous. Do not be afraid; do not be discouraged, for the LORD *your God will be with you wherever you go.*

Joshua 1:9

Slowly, but surely, she felt peace return. *The Bible describes it as "peace that passes understanding." How true,* she thought. *For as much as we have been through, it makes no sense for me to have peace about it. And I do, most of the time, even though I have to fight for it.*

As she locked the door and headed to her car, her mind traveled once again over the past eighteen years and the long journey she and Mitch had traveled.

Her memory took her to their first year of marriage. After just three months of marriage they began talking about having a baby. In fact, they never really had taken any measures to prevent having a baby. She was so young then. Most of her thoughts centered on baby bedding and tiny clothes. She thought about where she wanted to put a swing set in the back yard. She thought about learning to smock and what color she would paint the nursery. None of those kinds of things ever entered her mind now. She didn't care what color the nursery would be. She didn't care if it was a boy or a girl. Now she thought of the simplistic joy of simply holding a baby she knew was hers, one who would not be handed over to someone else when the obligatory ten minutes was over. She had definitely matured. Not that the other stuff would not be fun. It just didn't seem to matter as much now.

She remembered the first conversation that she and Mitch had about their fertility issues. It was early one morning and Peggy was, once again, on her period. Mitch was still sleeping and she scooted up next to him, feeling the warmth of his body spooned next to hers.

"Do you think there is a problem?" she said quietly. No reply except deep breathing.

"Mitch, are you awake?" she asked a bit louder.

"Huh?" he said sleepily.

"Do you think there is a problem?" she asked again.

"I don't know," was his reply. He didn't need further explanation as to the subject of her question. He wanted a baby as much as she did, and he wondered too, but had never wanted to voice his question. Somehow speaking it out loud seemed to make it more possible.

"Let's wait a while. If nothing happens, we will make an appointment with your doctor and see what he says," Mitch replied, ending the discussion.

No more was said that day, though the same conversation would come up many times. Years later, after two surgeries for Mitch and one surgery for Peggy, they gave up trying to have a baby on their own. Even the surgeries were just a stab in the dark. They never fixed the problem, nor even identified its real cause.

At least, after all these years they had narrowed their path to their child. They knew after so many failed procedures that the physical route to a baby was not going to happen. *When was it that we had finally accepted this fact?* she wondered. *I think it was about year ten, when we had tried every possible procedure, with all the needles and medicines and calendar watching.*

After ten years, they had tried everything and had practically bankrupted themselves. At that point, at the suggestion of their doctor, they had turned to the option of adoption. For eight years, that had been much of the focus of their life.

Their life was very different from what Peggy had imagined when she first fell in love with Mitch. They met in college, and it didn't take long to realize that their attraction to each other was deep and true, pure and right. Mitch was tall, athletic, and funny. His quick wit and good-natured sarcasm had carried the couple through many dark days. Peggy was sweet and strong, short and spunky—a rare mix of traits, which Mitch had always loved. They were still deeply in love, after all these years. They both were happy, most of the time, anyway. But neither felt complete. It was if there was a missing piece to their family. Yes, they went on with jobs they both enjoyed, sharing an office at a local real estate agency. And they enjoyed hobbies such as running and golf. As often as they could afford, they went to any and all sporting events for the University of Tennessee, their alma mater. Their lives were indeed full of many good things, just not with what they wanted the most—a child to hold and love. This journey to their child was ever pressing on both of their hearts and their minds.

As is often the case, Peggy carried the brunt of the weight of their struggle. It was her body that had been most often poked and prodded over the years. It felt like her failure. She knew that Mitch carried the same weight of "what if" and "why." He, too, felt it was his failure.

After Peggy's failed surgery—their last resort—both came home and cried. They grieved the loss of never being pregnant and physically having a baby, but soon moved on to the next challenge—the adoption process. If it were not for their faith in the wonderful sovereignty of God, they would have surely despaired. Just as God had created the world with just a spoken word, He was able to make Peggy pregnant by just speaking the command. And even still, He could bring a pretty little basket with a baby inside right to their doorstep, if He so chose. The issue was not *could* He, but *would* He?

And, so far, the fact that He had not was the struggle of their faith. However, rather than letting this struggle turn them away from their God, it made them run toward Him with every ounce of strength they had.

For Peggy, only when she figuratively crawled up in the lap of God and allowed Him to hold her with His arms of love did she feel any peace or acceptance of her situation. It was there she gained the strength she needed to try again and continue to wait.

Chapter 4

Tricia finally finished unpacking her garbage bags. There were a few extras in the bag, which she was surprised to see—a laundry bag with her name on it, new pens and pencils, new toiletries. Nothing huge, but it did indicate that maybe her mom cared about her a little bit. *Well, maybe not. Maybe she was just really ready for me to leave,* Tricia thought bitterly.

Though she had been on campus for two days now, she had hardly left her dorm room. She had been sent into exile here with no car, no extra spending money, and no promise of returning home until Thanksgiving break. So Tricia had no choice but to eat in the cafeteria on her pre-paid meal plan. She couldn't leave campus, and she knew no one. It had been a lonely two days. People seemed friendly enough, but Tricia just kept her head down when walking to the Student Union, and made sure she sat in a corner on the far end of the cafeteria. She wasn't ready to branch out just yet. What she really wanted was a cigarette. Better yet, a little bit of pot would really make her feel better. But her parents had made it very hard for her to obtain anything like that. *Unless of course, I make some friends who could take me off campus,* she thought. *Yep, that's what I am going to have to do. Make some friends.*

So Tricia finished the last bit of unpacking, checked her make-up, and left the safety of her dorm room to check out the campus. Just as she was locking her room, she heard the hall phone ringing. She certainly wasn't going to answer it. She didn't know anyone anyway.

As she was walking down the hall, she heard a cheery voice say, "Hello! Bethany Hall." After a brief pause she heard, "I don't know her, but let me check." Then, a very loud "Hey! Anybody know a Tricia Johnson? Her mom's on the phone!" Silence. Of course no one knew her. And she was certainly not going to talk to her mother right now—maybe never. She just kept on walking, a little bit quicker than before as if she were fleeing from an enemy. And that was what her parents were: her enemies. Out of nowhere, the phrase "love your enemies" popped into her mind. *No way. Not ready to go back to obeying scripture,* she thought. *I am too far gone now.* As if a movie reel was rolling in her head, scenes of her life in the past year flitted across her mind. Smoking, drinking, a little bit of drugs.

And then there was the "biggy," in her mind. The boys. How did she get there? That was one thing that she had never intended to do. Not before she was happily married to her prince charming. How did she get to this place in her life? Jake. Well, she couldn't totally blame him, but he was the beginning of her downfall.

Jake Rogers was a freshman at the University of

Tennessee. Being from Knoxville, Tricia had often met college guys from UT. But none had charmed her like Jake. He was smart, good-looking, and fun. She really just wanted to have fun. She didn't even love him. But somehow, when she spent more and more time with him, and less and less time with the Lord, her views changed. He was not a Christian; in fact, he didn't believe in anything but himself. He was an atheist and in time, his adamant insistence that there was no God, had definitely affected her relationship with her God. But she had had too many sweet, intimate times with Him to totally discount Him altogether.

Jake lived in a house with other UT students and there were non-stop parties. Every time Tricia entered the house, the mixed aromas of beer, cigarette smoke, salvaged furniture, and stale food assaulted her sense of smell. More often than not hung-over students reclined on the old, smelly sofas, sleeping off their latest party. At first Tricia felt uncomfortable in this setting, but in time, she fit right in. She soon could drink with the best of them and found that she also had an affinity for marijuana. Even with all of these new choices, she had not intended to lose her virginity. It just sort of happened. She hated herself for it.

Her memory took her back to the day of what she viewed as her biggest mistake. Afterwards, she went outside and sat on the picnic table in his backyard and cried her eyes out. After that, it seemed pointless to resist. She was already "stained." She was sure her youth group friends were speculating about her, and her parents were convinced that she was a "bad girl," so why fight it? Why not just be what they assumed? And so she was.

If only she had gone on to college when she was supposed to go. She received a piano and violin scholarship to Elliot University, where she now found herself, right out of high school. But she was scared. She convinced her parents to let her stay home and work for a year before she went to college. Big mistake. All her other big mistakes happened during that year. Only now they didn't seem like such big mistakes. Now, it was just the way it was.

This movie reel in her head brought with it the same nauseating feeling it always did. *I guess you could call it regret,* she thought. *But it is too late now. Can't go back and change it.*

She once thought she could. The day she finally broke up with Jake, she thought she could just forget the past and go back to her former faithful way of life. As she left Jake's house that day, she had put in her favorite praise and worship cassette tape. She sang at the top of her lungs, determined to change. That lasted about five hours.

That night, she had gone out with friends and plunged herself into a new level of unfaithfulness. Night after night for a solid month, she went out to party with her friends. Drinking, smoking pot, and leaving with the best-looking guys she could find had become her new way of life. *And that path would have continued if not for my controlling parents,* she thought with renewed anger.

Three nights ago, Tricia came home, drunk and high, at 2:00 in the morning. She discovered shortly after she arrived home that her parents were not asleep. Tricia walked down the hall to her bedroom, and to her surprise, it was filled with those ugly, black garbage bags. Everything she owned had been put in a bag. As she looked around her room in disbelief, her parents walked into the room. They looked cold, hard, and determined. They simply said, "Everything is packed. You are going to college. We will leave at 5:00 A.M." Tricia screamed and cursed and cried; then she pleaded and begged. But their minds were made up, and she had no choice but get in the car at 5:00. What a horrible trip that was. And Tricia made sure her parents were as miserable as she was for all 750 miles.

Replaying that scene added fuel to the angry fire in her heart. She walked faster down the hall, and then out the front doors of the dormitory. She wanted to get as far away as she could from that hall phone and her mother on the other end. She was now on a mission: Make a friend who had a car and could get her off this campus.

Chapter 5

Tricia's mom, Shirley Johnson, sat on the couch in the den with the portable phone lying in her lap. She looked straight ahead, staring into space. Though her eyes could have viewed the lovely surroundings of her beautiful but comfortable den, she saw none of it. No, right now her focus was on memories from long ago. She thought of her dear Tricia, so full of life, sitting at the baby grand piano, with legs pumping the piano pedals and fingers flying over the keys. She had on shorts and Converse® tennis shoes and a bandana over her messy hair. Shirley had bought her plenty of nicer clothes, but Tricia didn't seem to care about any of them. She just wanted her music. And talented she was, for sure. She could play the piano and the violin with such ease, that it made the instrument seem easy to play for others. Not that her giftedness had not required practice. Tricia practiced endlessly, but it was also effortless. She wanted to practice. She wanted to improve. Her love for music was beyond passionate. At that point, despite her young age, it was her life. Well, music and Jesus. Those were her two great passions.

Shirley turned her attention to her surroundings. So many memories, mostly happy, had taken place in this room. She could picture holidays, family devotions, and the everyday moments of living life, which had taken place over the past twenty years. All four of her children had come home from the hospital to this place. They had gone from Tinker Toys® to rock music, so quickly. She lovingly thought of each of her children when they were indeed children—April, Tricia, Wayne, and Wendy. They were all teenagers now. Sometimes she longed for the days when they were little and loved their mom. Each child had presented various obstacles to overcome, but never anything too difficult or devastating. Until now.

She looked toward the fireplace, and then to the baby grand piano beside it. It almost seemed out of place in this lovely but modest room. They were a middle class family who had sometimes struggled to raise four children. But God always provided, and they always had enough, for which they were continually grateful. The shiny, black baby grand was a great luxury indeed. She thought back to the day it arrived. It was really for Tricia, though the whole family enjoyed it. As Tricia's fifteenth birthday rolled around, they considered buying her a car. But music was what was really important in Tricia's world, much more than the typical teenager's desire for freedom and wheels. So they decided that instead of a car, they would get a piano. The fact that it was a baby grand was the big surprise. But they had wanted the very best for their talented daughter. *Tricia. What happened? How did she change so quickly? If only we could go back.*

This train of thought immediately took her to another scene from the past. She and Tricia, along with Lloyd and their other children, had sat in this very room together reading from the Bible. Lloyd had read a certain passage—*What was it?--- Ephesians 2, I think it was. Yes, that was it.* Her biblical knowledge gained over 30 years of seeking Him proved faithful to bring the passage to mind with exact words.

> *But because of his great love for us, God, who is rich in mercy, made us alive with Christ even when we were dead in transgressions—it is by grace you have been saved. And God raised us up with Christ and seated us with him in the heavenly realms in Christ Jesus, in order that in the coming ages he might show the incomparable riches of his grace, expressed in his kindness to us in Christ Jesus. For it is by grace you have been saved, through faith—and this not from yourselves, it is the gift of God— not by works, so that no one can boast. For we are God's workmanship, created in Christ Jesus to do good works, which God prepared in advance for us to do.*
>
> *Ephesians 2:4-9*

The memory was so vivid that she could even now, a decade later, recall practically word for word what had been said. Lloyd read from the passage. He began to explain what grace is: God's Riches At Christ's Expense. He explained that God gives His mercy and grace in offering salvation to each of us. We surely don't deserve it. We certainly could never earn it. Only Jesus, by paying the price of it by dying on the cross, could provide grace to us. He focused on verse 8, *"For it is by grace you have been saved, through faith—and it is not of yourselves, it is a gift of God."* Lloyd then spoke with great joy of salvation being the greatest gift of all. They closed in prayer and then all sang *Amazing Grace* together. April, Tricia, and Wayne all sat on the couch. Shirley held Wendy, who was just a toddler. Tricia sat on the end of the couch, closest to her mom. As they sang the wonderful, powerful song, Shirley looked over at her three older children. Joy welled up in her heart. And then she noticed seven-year-old, Tricia. In her mind's eye, she could clearly see that look on her face, even now. Tears had filled her beautiful, green eyes. Though normally loud and fidgety, Tricia was perfectly still. As the song came to a close, Shirley leaned over to her daughter and asked, "Tricia, honey, are you okay?"

A slight nod of the head was her only response.

Unconvinced, Shirley persisted, "Are you sure? I can tell something is bothering you."

Tricia looked at her mother and simply said, "I want that. I want that grace that Daddy was talking about. I want Jesus."

Shirley looked at her husband and both smiled. "Well, honey, we can take care of that right now, if you think you are ready."

Tricia nodded and said, "I'm ready."

As often takes place between husband and wife, silent communication flowed between them. In their opinion, leading your child to Christ was the ultimate privilege, and Lloyd gave that as a gift to his wife. He walked over and took Wendy from Shirley's arms. Shirley then got up and took Tricia's hand and both knelt beside the chair and prayed a simple prayer of repentance and faith: *Jesus, I know that You are holy and perfect and good, and I am not. I am sorry for the wrong things that I do. I need You to save me. Please forgive all of my sins, and come and live in my heart. Thank You for saving me, Jesus. Amen.* And so Tricia's spiritual journey had begun.

Shirley remembered that over the next several years, Tricia grew in her love for her Lord and Savior. *Heaven knows, we did everything in our power to "instruct her and teach her in the way that she should go," like it says in Proverbs. We took her to church every time the doors were open. We taught her Scripture, sent her to a Christian school, prayed with her and for her. What else could we have done, Lord?* Shirley silently prayed, as bitter tears, unshed, stung her eyes.

What about that promise at the end of that verse, Lord? "And in the end, they will not depart from it." That is what You said, Lord. And yet, Tricia has departed from what we have taught her. She has departed from who she is, who You mean for her to be, and honestly, who I wanted her to be. I don't even know her any more.

Shirley resisted the urge to cry. No, she didn't want to do that right now. The bitterness in her spirit was so raw that if she allowed herself to give in to the tears, she would cry the whole day. *No, that won't do. I have too much on my list today to spend it crying over what I can't change,* she thought bitterly. *I have given that girl enough tears for now.* And yet, Shirley couldn't seem to move. She didn't cry, but she continued to sit and stare and think of better days and what could have been.

She was still sitting there an hour later when Lloyd came home for lunch. He walked into the room and roused her from her trance. He saw the phone lying in her lap. He saw the look on her face. He realized, not for the first time, that these problems with Tricia had aged his lovely wife. The spark was gone from her eyes and the lines across her forehead were deeper and more prominent. She was still beautiful, but there was a heaviness of spirit that she now carried that he wished he could take away from her. But he couldn't, for his own heaviness was far too much for him to carry right now as it was. At least they were on the same page. Adding the stress of opposite opinions would have really sent him over the edge.

Piecing together the phone in her lap and the look on her face, he asked, "Did you get in touch with her?"

"No," she said dejectedly.

"She won't avoid us forever," he replied, wanting desperately to offer encouragement to his heartbroken wife.

"I am not so sure about that," she said.

"We did the right thing," Lloyd said with conviction.

"Yes, we did the right thing."

Chapter 6

Elliot University was a small, private Christian college, located in Orange Grove, Florida, a city of about 50,000 located midway between Tampa and Orlando—In other words, a long way from Tricia's home in Knoxville, Tennessee. Palm trees, orange groves, and sparkling lakes enhanced the beautiful, 87-acre campus. Of the 2,950 students that attended the university, approximately 70 percent lived on campus. All of these students professed to be Christians. Or at least, like Tricia, their parents did. *Surely, there are others like me who fit into a different mold than the straight-laced, Bible-believing and Bible-living mold that most adhere to here,* she had thought more than once in the past two days.

The mantra of the school was "Be Strong. Be Wise. Be Salt." Salt was right. Being there felt like salt in the wounds of Tricia's heart. In August of 1991, Tricia found it to be the prison she would be sentenced to for four long years. Looking forward, all she saw were strict rules and goody-goody people like her parents. She could hardly imagine how she used to fit in with this type of crowd. That was before. Now, it just felt like prison.

As Tricia left Bethany Hall, fleeing the phone call from her mother, she was greeted with dry, hot air. *At least there is a warm breeze. The humidity is not nearly as bad as it is in Knoxville right now,* she thought. And indeed, she was right, as Orange Grove, Florida had a semitropical climate with an average annual temperature of 72 degrees. She walked down the sidewalk, toward the Student Union. She made an effort to keep her head up and make eye contact. She saw friendly faces, many of which had that certain "light" in their eyes, the light for which she had once been known. She thought to herself, *Mental Checklist: Avoid the ones who are too chipper, too willing to look me straight in the eyes. They wouldn't be the type of friends who would help me in my predicament.*

As she continued her trek across campus, she saw Mediterranean-style architecture adorned with Queen Palm trees, lush green space, and blooming flowers in manicured beds along the walkway. Closer to the Student Union benches and picnic tables were scattered around. As Tricia passed the area, she heard a small group of students—one with a guitar—discussing their favorite music. Tricia recognized every name of the Christian artists mentioned. That used to be her "thing." She knew every word to every song Amy Grant and Sandi Patti had ever recorded. And yet, that did not make her feel any "oneness" with those students. Instead, ironically, it made her feel more isolated. If they only knew…

As she entered the Student Union she heard the

student with the guitar strum the beginning cords of "Healing Love," a popular contemporary worship song. Just a year ago, Tricia would have stopped and joined in. Today, it just made her walk faster, away from the sound, away from her past.

She opened the door, and bumped into a handsome, dark-haired guy. She looked up to see a set of very blue eyes, with a surprised, concerned look.

"I'm so sorry. Are you okay?" he said in reference to their abrupt encounter.

"Yeah, I'm fine. No problem," she replied.

With that, his face lit up into a wide and wonderful smile. "I don't think we have met. I'm Shane Robbins."

"I'm Tricia. Tricia Johnson."

"Well, it's nice to meet you.You must be a freshman."

"Yeah. What about you?"

"I'm a junior. You're going to love it here. Just get involved on campus. Everyone is really nice."

"Yeah. Well, I better go."

"Okay. See you later. Nice to meet you."

"See you later."

Just as Shane walked away, Jessica Kincade walked up and greeted Tricia. Jessica was Tricia's HELP leader. HELP stood for Help and Encouragement Learning Pod. The university was committed to making the transition for incoming freshman as pleasant as possible. They arranged for every freshman to be a part of a HELP team, which offered the opportunity for eight to twelve new friends right away and helped them ease into the academic community. They were gender-separated small groups formed to give freshmen a little extra support, and in Tricia's case, a little extra irritation.

During orientation, Tricia had met Jessica as well as the other members of her HELP group. Jessica was tiny in height and weight, with long, straight brown hair, which was usually pulled back in a pony-tail. She was out-going, fun, and full of energy. Her vivacous personality and cute appearance made her a perfect example of a HELP leader. Though at first glance Jessica appeared shallow, further examination of her character revealed a depth of insight, compassion, and strong leadership skills. Every Monday the upper-class leader was supposed to meet with the team and guide discussions about issues such as relationships, procrastination, and fear. It was supposed to be a growth opportunity to develop character and leadership skills. Tricia wanted nothing to do with the group.

"I see you met Shane Robbins," Jessica said, flashing a knowing smile. "Cute, isn't he?"

When Tricia didn't reply, she continued. "He's sort of a 'big man on campus.' Great, Christian guy. Student Government treasurer. He is a good friend of mine. He smiled alot when talking to you," she said that last sentence with a teasing, sing-song tone of voice. Tricia ignored the implication.

"Yeah, he seems nice," she simply replied. Changing the subject as quickly as possible, Tricia said, "Oh, uh, sorry I missed the meeting the other night. I wasn't feeling very well."

"That's okay. Just glad to see that you're feeling better. Let me know if you need anything." And with that Tricia and her only semi-friend, parted ways. Tricia quickly ate lunch, by herself, and then retreated back to the safety of her dorm room in Bethany Hall.

Chapter 7

Peggy parallel parked in front of their office building. Just as she was about to unbuckle and go inside to get Mitch, the passenger side door opened, startling her.

"Oh, Mitch! Gosh, honey, you scared me!"

"A little on edge today, huh?" Mitch replied.

"No, I just didn't expect you to jump right in." She paused for just a second, and then confessed, "Okay, well, maybe I am a bit on edge. I guess I'm just nervous about this meeting. Jane said she had something she wanted to talk to us about in person. With our track record, that can't be good news. I'm trying not to care… but I do."

"I know. Me too," he replied.

They rode in silence, both lost in their own thoughts for the rest of the drive to New Life Adoption Agency, a place with which they had both become very familiar. They had started their journey to adoption with this agency, and even though nothing had worked out yet, they were comfortable with the people who worked there.

Jane Crosby was their caseworker. She had been with them from the beginning, and had walked with them through some intensely sad and stressful times. She had become a dear friend to both of them. Jane was the one who helped guide them through the mounds of paperwork for their homestudy, the group of documents needed to prove that Mitch and Peggy were worthy of becoming adoptive parents. The homestudy contained information of almost everything in their lives: birth certificates, financial statements, recommendations from friends and co-workers, background checks, health reports, fingerprints, and on and on and on. Jane also was the person who had facilitated their home visit. The home visit took place in the adoption process when much of the application work had been completed, and was necessary for confirming a healthy and safe environment in the home. They were visited by Jane so she could examine their homelife.

Looking back, Peggy realized she might have gone a bit overboard for the homestudy. She had cleaned out closets and the attic, washed baseboards, made Mitch touch up paint throughout the house, and made sure there were cookies baking in the oven and fresh flowers on the table the day Jane came. She knew now it was unnecessary to go to all the trouble, but at the time it was as if Peggy was nesting. Though she had never been pregnant, she had heard her friends talk of the phenomenon of "nesting," the almost uncontrollable urge to clean and prepare the "nest" for the new baby, just prior to birth. She had known of foolish friends who climbed ladders, painted rooms, and cleaned out garages, just hours before they went into labor. And what her fertile friends described, she actually felt, too, when preparing for their homestudy. At the time, she thought surely it was a "sign" that they would be placed with a baby soon. *Surely, I am at the end of this long, long "pregnancy,"* she had thought. Sadly, her "pregnancy" had continued for years.

For just a moment, her mind traveled backwards in time, briefly stopping on each failed adoption. Four times in the past four years, a young, unwed mother had interviewed and chosen Peggy and Mitch to become the adoptive parents of the baby she carried. Each time, the birth mother had changed her mind. The first failed adoption was the most devastating.

Peggy remembered vividly what she wore that day. It seemed important when she dressed for the meeting with Jane. She spent much time sorting through her clothes, wondering what most looked like a loving mother. She set aside her business attire, as well as her jeans, and settled on a nice black skirt and brightly colored sweater. She knew they were getting very close to the due date. She thought the purpose of the meeting was to prepare them for the process of bringing their child home. *Maybe the time is already here. Maybe Jane is going to take us to the hospital,* she thought excitedly, but then realized it didn't seem likely that they would first go to her office instead of meeting at the hospital.

Peggy and Mitch entered Jane's office feeling nervous, but extremely excited. They took one look at Jane's face and they knew something was wrong.

"What? What's wrong, Jane?" Peggy said, not waiting to sit down first.

"Peggy and Mitch, we have a problem. The couple has reunited. The boyfriend is back in Heather's life and promises to stay by her side and help her raise the baby."

"He won't stay. He hasn't wanted anything to do with Heather in months. He took off right after she told him she was pregnant," Mitch said, frustration pouring forth with every word.

"And he hit her. Heather told me," Peggy added with growing despair.

"I know. I agree. But we can't prove the abuse and Heather now denies it. Plus, according to Tennessee law, birth parents have a grace period in which they can change their minds. They are within that period. We can't do anything about it. I am so sorry," Jane replied, clearly upset as well.

And thus began their painful experience with adoption—hoping, waiting, then grieving. *Surely God will not let us suffer like this forever,* Peggy had often thought with each passing year.

As her thoughts focused back on the task at hand, Peggy could only hope this meeting with Jane would not be stressful. They parked in front of the New Life Adoption Agency and went together, hand in hand, into the familiar building. That is why they had survived so many disappointments. They always went through life hand in hand, literally and figuratively.

Peggy and Mitch had met in college. They started out as very good friends. Their friendship developed over time into a deep love that many of their friends envied. One of Peggy's friends had once, confidentially, asked her, "How are you two so close? I see what you and Mitch have together and I want that for my marriage."

Peggy had nodded in understanding. She had never really compared her marriage to others', but in that moment, she understood her friend's question. She replied, "Yes, Mitch and I are very close. I would like to say that we are just the fairy tale couple. But the truth is, it's been the hardship in our lives that have joined us so tightly together. Without the hardship, the really, really difficult times, I think we would be just like most couples. But when life is difficult you have a choice. It can make you stronger, closer, and more intimate, or it can tear you apart. We chose to draw together, with God's help. That is why we are so close."

Still holding hands, they entered Jane's office. Jane greeted them warmly, immediately putting them at ease. After they were all comfortably seated, Jane got right to the point.

"I asked you both to come in today because I had another call from a lawyer friend who has a client who wants to put her baby up for adoption. The baby is due in 6 months. The reason that I wanted to talk about this in person is because of your past disappointments. To be honest, I have never heard of a couple going through what you two have gone through, and I've been at this for over twenty years. I just wanted to make sure you two still want to try. This is another risk, for sure. Maybe even more than before. My lawyer friend doesn't know his client very well; she is from North Carolina. I'm not sure how she got to Knoxville. I know you both are very strong. I know your faith is very strong. But, truthfully, with each of your failed adoptions, I have felt a bit responsible."

Peggy was the first to reply, and Mitch nodded his agreement as she spoke. "Jane, none of those situations was your fault. I don't understand it, but we have never blamed you or this agency."

"Thanks for saying that. And as I have gone through each situation over and over in my mind, I don't think we should have necessarily done anything differently. But I have grown to love you both, and I don't want to see you hurt again."

Peggy looked at Mitch and communicated without words. Mitch spoke this time. "Normally, we would tell you that we will pray about it. But, you know, we have prayed about it for 18 years. And God hasn't released us from the desire to have a child. So, until He does, I guess we just keep trying."

Peggy nodded and smiled, though the smile did not quite reach her eyes. She was scared. But not too scared to try again.

"Okay, then. That is what I needed to hear," Jane replied. And with that, she picked up the phone and dialed the lawyer's number.

Chapter 8

Tricia and her roommate, Susan, got along just fine. Tricia kept to herself and avoided unnecessary conversation. Susan had jumped right into college life, with all its various activities, and therefore was rarely in the room. Susan had tried at first to befriend her, but the wall surrounding Tricia's heart prevented true friendship. Now, two weeks into the semester, they had settled into a workable routine. They weren't really friends, but they weren't close enough to fight either. They just happened to live in the same 12' 6" x 12' room, and both made the most of it. They each had a twin bed, dresser, closet, desk, and chair. Tricia kept her stuff on her side of the room, and Susan kept her stuff on the other side. Tricia doubted they would be roommates next year, maybe not even next semester. But it was a workable situation for now.

Tricia had not gotten to know anyone, although that was more her fault than the fault of the other students. Elliot University was a friendly campus, in both students and faculty.

Her mission to find a friend who would take her off campus proved futile. Everyone was just too nice to approach with that kind of request.

Her HELP group was designed to assist freshman in meeting new people, but Tricia had avoided the first two meetings, due to "illness." That is what she told her team leader, Jessica, anyway. And it wasn't really a lie, either. Tricia did feel ill at the time. In fact, Tricia felt ill a lot lately. And she was tired—really, really tired. But she knew she couldn't give another excuse when the next HELP team meeting rolled around.

HELP teams met in dorms, conference and class rooms on campus, and occasionally off campus. Attendance at HELP team meetings earned required chapel credits. Three mornings each week, the whole campus was required to get a spiritual boost from chapel service, which consisted of worship and a message. The campus choirs and bands or other college musicians led the worship. The message was given by professors or guest speakers. The university required an unbelievable number of chapel credits per semester. If attendance was consistent at HELP team meetings, more excused absences were allowed for chapel. That is what really motivated Tricia to go to the meeting.

Jessica had left a cute little note, complete with a smiley face, on Tricia's door, letting her know the time and place of the meeting—6:00 P.M. in room 606 of the Science building, Monday, of course. As Tricia was brushing her teeth, a little before six that Monday night, she longed to call in sick again. And she did feel sick again. It seemed almost daily she felt a slight queasiness, especially at night. *I'm just tired,* she thought. *Funny though, I spent the past year partying all night, every night, and I didn't feel this tired.*

Suddenly, she stopped brushing her teeth, mid-brush. A cold, nauseating feeling came across her as a thought popped into her head. *What if I'm pregnant?* Her heart suddenly pounded in her chest. *No, it can't be that. There is a reason it's called morning sickness, isn't there? I have been feeling sick more at night.* With that more reasonable thought, Tricia's heart slowed its furious beating just a little bit. That is, until, the next thought popped in her head. *Wait a minute.... When was my last period? I can't remember. Seems like it has been a while. Oh, God! What if I'm pregnant?* And with that, Tricia really was sick.

OOOOOOO

Tricia rushed into room 606 in the Science building fifteen minutes late. She expected to see disapproving looks from the other prompt students, but instead, she was greeted with genuine smiles. They actually seemed glad to see her. Jessica patiently paused the meeting to reintroduce everyone to Tricia. She had met them all once before, but that was two weeks ago, and she couldn't remember a single name. The meeting was tolerable, not near as boring as she imagined. In fact, in her former life, she would have actually enjoyed it. Some of the girls seemed like "friend-material." Just as that thought surfaced, it was immediately replaced by another: *But, what if I'm pregnant? Any hope of making friends in this place would be gone, for sure. In fact, I am sure that I would get kicked out of school. Oh, I can't be pregnant! I just can't!*

"Tricia, are you okay?" The question brought her back to the present. It was the end of the meeting and everyone was gathering their things to leave. Tricia, lost in those disturbing thoughts, continued to sit there, staring into space. The question was from Jessica, but a couple of the other girls were looking at her with concern.

"Oh, yeah. Sorry. I guess I'm tired. Yes, I'm fine. Thanks."

"Spiritual Emphasis Week starts tomorrow. Supposed to be a great speaker. It's in the chapel tomorrow night at 6. Wanna go?" When Tricia hesitated, Jessica continued, "It is a good chance to get ahead with your chapel credits. That may help later in the semester, when you have more going on, and need to skip a service or two. Don't you wanna go?"

"Sure. I'll go," Tricia reluctantly replied, with an insincere smile on her face.

"Great! I'll come by your dorm room around 5:45 and we can walk over together."

"Okay. Thanks."

"See you then!" And with that, Jessica bounced off to some other freshman to cheer and mentor. Tricia, on the other hand, walked slowly back to the dorm, with the familiar nauseating feeling growing stronger with each step, as the horrible thought rolled over and over in her mind: *What if I'm pregnant?*

Chapter 9

Peggy was cooking dinner when Mitch came home. She greeted him in the usual way, asking about his day at work, telling him about her day. She continued to prepare the meal as they talked. Not until they sat down at the kitchen table to eat did she notice he seemed distracted, maybe a bit nervous.

"Is something wrong, Mitch?" she asked with concern.

"No, nothing is wrong, but there is something that I need to tell you. I'm not sure how you'll feel about it."

"What is it? Just say it."

"I talked to your mom today. She called me at work. She called to tell me that Vicky is pregnant." He paused to gauge her response. She just sat there in silence looking at him. Then she looked down at her hands.

"Why didn't she call *me*?" she asked.

"Well, she didn't know how you would react. They know our struggle, honey. They share it, too. Your mom just thought that you would rather hear it from me first, before you talked to any of them."

Without another word, Peggy burst into tears. Mitch got up from his place at the table, took her hand, and led her to the couch. Then he just held her. He didn't have to say anything. There was nothing to say.

Vicky was Peggy's baby sister. Peggy was eight years older than Vicky. And now she was going to have a baby. Her baby sister would be a mom before Peggy would. Peggy wanted to be happy for her. It wasn't that she didn't want Vicky to have a child. It's just that it seemed so unfair. To top it off, the whole family felt like they had to walk on eggshells around her. Her own mother couldn't call her to tell her the big family news. *God, what about me?*

The next day Peggy still felt angry and bitter. She didn't know who she was angry with. Vicky? Her mom? God? Maybe all of them. She did work up the courage and fake enthusiasm to call her mom and Vicky to tell them both how happy she was with the news. *Yeah, right.*

That afternoon, Peggy got a call at work from Jane.

"Hey, Peggy! I just wanted to touch base with you about the new birth mother. Her name is Carla. As we already know, she is originally from North Carolina. She has lived here in Knoxville for about three years."

Quick to think through complications, Peggy asked,

"What about the birth father?"

"The birth father has signed the papers to waive his parental rights, so that is a non-issue."

"Okay. What next?"

"Now, we just need to set up a time to meet her. After that, she will decide if you two are the ones to raise this child. You know the drill. I, nor the agency, nor the lawyer can make any promises. But it does seem positive. What do you think?"

"I think this is good news. And that is the way I will take it, until I have reason to think otherwise. I will check with Mitch's schedule and call you back," Peggy responded cheerfully. As she hung up the phone, the dark cloud that had surrounded her since the night before slowly began to lift.

Chapter 10

Tricia heard a sharp knock on her dorm room door at exactly 5:45 Monday evening. *Of course, she would be right on time,* Tricia thought sarcastically. She opened the door and plastered a fake smile on her face. Jessica greeted her warmly, reminded her to bring her Bible, and waited patiently while she found it. Tricia was slightly embarrassed that it took so long to locate it. Obviously, she had not picked it up in quite a while. But Tricia knew the "talk of the walk," and could certainly use the language of Christianity well enough to fool anyone. When she finally found her Bible in the bottom of her closet, she grabbed her purse and locked the door behind her.

She and Jessica walked quickly to the chapel. A guest evangelist would be the speaker, and a guest praise band would lead the worship. She dreaded it. She hoped that both the band and the evangelist would keep an eye on the clock. They entered the double doors of the chapel, and found the place already packed. But Jessica had friends. She managed to secure two seats half-way down the aisle, on the right end. Tricia happened to glance to her left as she walked down the aisle and spotted Shane Robbins. He saw her too and sent a smile her way. She smiled briefly and quickly looked away. *I am not interested. No way. He is too nice for me. Too good.*

She settled into her seat and was glad the music started right away so she wouldn't have to continue to make small talk with Jessica. At first, the music was instrumental. Though she didn't want to admit it, the sound filled her senses, causing her to experience just a bit of her former peace. She heard the rise and fall of each note, and felt an urge to play along. Instead, she closed her eyes and drank in the sound. Soon, beautiful voices mingled together with words so pure, so true that the hard corners of her heart began to melt. She felt, well, *homesick* would be the best word to describe it. She was not homesick for her mom or her house or Knoxville. She realized with great surprise that she was homesick for Him—her God, her First Love, the One she had walked away from. *Can I go back?* she wondered with longing. They all stood and sang several worship songs together. Tricia knew every one. For the first time in a long, long time, she sincerely meant what she sang. *Can I go back?* she wondered again.

Soon, the students were settled back in their seats and waited for the evangelist to begin. Tricia felt disappointed. She did not want the music to end, or this renewed feeling of peace to end. But her disappointment quickly faded as the words of the evangelist fell like a healing balm to her wounded soul. Later, when she thought back on the evening, she couldn't really remember all that the preacher had said.

But what she did remember was the scripture he read.

But he was pierced for our rebellion,
crushed for our sins.
He was beaten so we could be whole.
He was whipped so we could be healed.
Isaiah 53:5, NLT

Tricia had heard those words many times before, but she had never *needed* them to be true the way she needed them that night. The thought of all the ugliness of the past months being taken off of her and put on Jesus caused both relief and grief. Relief in that maybe, just maybe, she could find a way out of the mess of her life. Grief because she knew the darkness of her sin. And Jesus was so pure, so perfect. She could hardly bear to think of her darkness being put on His pure light.

When the sermon ended, the evangelist opened the altar for a time of prayer. Tricia was the first one down. She found the least conspicuous place possible, to the far right. She knelt at the altar, with her hands and head leaning on the rail. Then the tears came. She couldn't stop them and she didn't even try. She wept and wept. She wept over the mistakes she had made, she wept over the grief she had caused, and she wept over the brokenness of her mind, body, and spirit, the result of her defiant choices. In the quietness of her heart, her prayer reached heaven's gate and rushed to the throne of God. She went boldly to the throne of grace as she prayed, *Oh, Jesus,*

I'm sorry. I'm so sorry. I am sorry for the sins that I willingly committed. You know them all. Even the memory of them makes me sick. Take it away from me, God. Restore me to You. Help me, Jesus. Please, Lord, help me. I want to come back to You, even though I am broken and stained. I'm so sorry, Jesus.

This repentance brought with it the reality of the ugliness of her choices, and at the same time brought hope that the broken pieces of her life could be made right again. She felt hope for the first time in a long time.

Unbeknownst to Tricia, Shane Robbins watched her and prayed for her the whole time she knelt at the altar. He was drawn to her in a way he did not understand. Yes, she was beautiful, for sure—her light brown hair, green eyes, and beautiful smile would surely be noticed by any guy. But it was more than that. He would just have to ask the Lord about it.

As Tricia and Jessica walked back to the dorm after the service, Tricia felt lighter than she had in many months. Still, so many questions and fears tumbled in her mind, but the hope remained.

Jessica awkwardly broached the subject of Tricia's experience at the chapel service as they neared Bethany Hall.

"Tricia, I saw how moved you were tonight at the service. I don't know what's going on in your life—and I don't need to know anything at all. I just wanted to say that if you need a friend to talk to…well, just know that you can call me any time, okay?" Jessica almost seemed relieved to have gotten that out. Tricia understood. It is never easy to get into someone else's problems, especially if you aren't sure whether they want you there.

Tricia sensed that this gentle prying was truly sincere. She responded sincerely, too. "Thanks, Jessica. My life is very complicated right now. But I think that tonight I made a step in the right direction."

As Tricia laid down that night, with her Bible now on the table beside her bed instead of in the bottom of her closet, she slept peacefully for the first time in many months.

Chapter 11

On Wednesday, Tricia still felt the warmth of her experience at the altar. She got up, read her Bible, showered, and then headed toward the Student Union to grab some breakfast before class. On her way there she saw Shane walking toward her. As he neared, he flashed her that beautiful smile and his blue eyes lit up.

"I was hoping I would see you today," he said as approached her.

She didn't know what to make of that greeting, so she simply said, "Hi, Shane. How are you?"

"I'm good. Listen, I wondered if you might have some free time tonight for us to get together."

"Well, I'm not sure. I really need to study. And I really wanted to go to the chapel service tonight."

"Yeah, me, too. Maybe we could walk over to the service together and then find a place to study?" he said with a smile.

"Okay. I guess that would work," she replied hesitantly.

"Great. I'll come by your dorm a little before six tonight. Sound good?"

"Yeah, that's good. I'll see you then," she replied with a smile.

As they parted, her thoughts flew back and forth between, *"Bad idea, Tricia!"* to, *"This is no big deal."* Deep down, she knew she shouldn't be forming any type of friendship with this great guy. *It will only lead to disappointment for him and for me. I still might be pregnant, and then what?* she thought. She could only hope she would start her period soon. Then she would be able to really have a fresh start with a clean slate.

She thought about going to buy a pregnancy test, but without a car she couldn't get off campus. Those certainly weren't stocked in the school store in the Student Union, and she didn't have friends to take her. *If Kat were here, she would take me, for sure—and without condemnation,* she had thought on numerous occasions. Truthfully, as scary as not knowing was, at least she still had hope that she *wasn't* pregnant. *Maybe not having a chance to get a pregnancy test is not such a bad thing,* she reasoned.

Throughout the day, she was tempted to find Shane and make up an excuse to cancel her time with him that night. But she realized she didn't know which dorm he lived in. *If I run into him again, I'll tell him I'm not feeling well and cancel our plans. And it won't be a lie, either. I don't feel well.* She didn't see him again until he knocked on her door just before six.

"Sorry, I'm a little late," he said. He was breathing heavily, as if he had run the whole way.

"No problem. I'm ready. Just let me get my Bible." She quickly got it from her bedside table, grabbed her purse, locked the door, and they headed out.

Shane did most of the talking along the way. She couldn't help but enjoy herself. He was smart and funny and easy-going. A year ago, he would have been just the kind of guy that she would want—but a lot had changed in a year. She knew she could go back to Jesus, but it seemed awfully unfair to such a great guy like Shane to involve him in her complicated life. She decided to simply enjoy the time with him that night and cut off any further communication.

When they entered the chapel, once again, instrumental music played to set the tone of the evening. It was worshipful and wonderful and filled Tricia's senses. She felt at home in the sound. They quickly found a seat and prepared their hearts for worship. As the vocals began to accompany the music, Tricia sang along, eyes closed, heart open. At that moment she didn't care about anything but worshipping the One who had saved her and welcomed her home again. She didn't care about impressing Shane. She didn't care about what anyone else thought about her. She cared only about what He thought. Tears, once again, began to flow down her cheeks. She didn't even try to wipe them away. These tears were not the desperate tears of the previous night. No, these tears were tears of gratitude. Yes, she still had to deal with the possible consequences of her choices. But she would no longer be dealing with life alone. She had returned to the One who promised to never leave her or forsake her.

Shane worshiped, too, but he also could not help noticing Tricia beside him. She was beautiful in worship. Her voice, her countenance, her posture, and her total oblivion to what else was going on around her all blended together for a breathtaking sight. Her worship was sincere, heartfelt, and pure. Yes, the purity of it is what stood out most to him. *I've got a lot of praying to do about this girl,* Shane thought.

Another anointed sermon from the evangelist brought both knowledge and conviction to those who listened with open hearts. Tricia and Shane were included in the "open heart" category. As they walked to the library to study, they both enjoyed discussing what they learned and how they could apply it to their own lives. Shane talked the most, but Tricia shared, too, though her sharing was clothed in vague comments. Nothing too personal, as her past was in the past and that is where she wanted it to stay.

She had begun to wish the whole past year of her life could just be erased, as if it could be like a bad dream from which she awoke. In a bad dream, one awakes fearful, with heart pounding and sweat pouring. Then there is the moment of realization that it was really just a bad dream. All the dreadful things just experienced weren't real after all, therefore there is nothing to fear and nothing to deal with. She wished that could happen. But she knew better. *The past does come into the present. It doesn't have to control the present, but it does come. Only God's grace will help me learn to deal with my past in the present. Once dealt with, then it can be truly past—but not until I know if I am pregnant.*

After studying for a couple of hours, Shane walked Tricia back to Bethany Hall. Tricia was quiet as they walked. A subtle sadness seemed to wash over her. She would love to spend more time with Shane, but she knew that doing so would be to set up both of them for heartache. She could already tell that Shane liked her. She wished that she were free to like him back, but she wasn't. Not now. Maybe not ever. As they neared the front door of Bethany Hall, Shane suggested that they study together again the next night. Tricia made up an excuse as to why she couldn't. He knew it was a lame excuse and so did she.

He paused for just a moment, and then said, "Look Tricia, I know you don't know me very well. I'm not usually a pushy person, but I want to be your friend. I wish you would give me a chance to get to know you. I can be a pretty good friend if you give me a chance." With that he flashed a half smile her way, one that was hopeful and yet unsure. Tricia could not say no to that.

"Well, I guess I could use a friend," she replied quietly.

His smile grew wide and he said, "Okay. Then, see you tomorrow?"

"Yeah. See you tomorrow."

Thus began a friendship, deep and wonderful. And it was about to be thoroughly tested.

ooooooo

Tricia and Shane found themselves together a lot in the following days. Night after night they studied together, ate together in the cafeteria, and walked together around the beautiful campus, enjoying the warm, tropical breezes each evening. When they were together, Tricia could forget who she had been over the past year, and she could be who she longed to be. However, each night as she returned to the dorm, she was plagued with the reality that secrets are never secrets forever. She knew she was forgiven, but she also knew that poor choices came with painful consequences.

She tried to resist his constant invitations, but she couldn't. After two weeks, she knew he had deep feelings for her, and she wanted the freedom to return those feelings. But with each day that came and went without the start of her period, she became more certain that she was pregnant. However, it was so surreal, and her life was so different than it had been just a month ago, she found that she could stuff that possibility in a compartment of her heart, and not let it surface into reality. She began to share the feelings that Shane so readily showed. But in time, she began to care more about what was best for him, than about what she wanted with him.

She began to pull away as best she could. She wouldn't accept his calls, and she made up excuses for why she couldn't spend time with him. But she didn't know everything there was to know about Shane Robbins. She didn't know that he was "purely" stubborn. When Shane believed that God told him something, nothing could convince him otherwise. After much prayer, Shane believed that God had told him that Tricia was the girl for him. He dared not say "love"—it was too soon for that—but deep in the recesses of his heart, that is what he felt. So he continued to pursue.

Finally, one day Tricia sat him down on a park bench

on campus. She chose a place where few would pass by. She sat cross-legged on the bench facing Shane. With as much sincerity and clarity as she could muster, she said, "Shane, I am not the girl for you. You have to hear me on this. I am not who you think I am. I have been a bad, party girl for quite a while. You deserve better than that." As the words came out of her mouth, they seemed to take a piece of her heart with them. She knew after hearing that, this great Christian man before her would graciously accept the fact that they were not meant to be.

Shane looked at Tricia and said, "I think you better let me be the judge of that."

The look on his face was one of challenge, as if he were saying, "*Bring it on. I can handle anything you've done.*" Tricia knew otherwise.

In frustration, she blurted out, "Listen to me. I think I am pregnant."

That statement brought a silence and a heaviness that broke Tricia's heart. They just stared at each other. Tears filled Tricia's eyes. She knew that did the trick. He was gone. She just hoped that he would be godly enough to keep her revelation to himself.

Shane ended the silence with words that brought confusion and unbelief to Tricia's ears and heart.

"Well, I'm going to fast and pray and ask the Lord what I am supposed to do," he said softly and sincerely.

"Fast and pray? You've got to be kidding me! Did you hear what I just said?" Tricia practically shouted at him.

"I heard you. Can I call you in a couple of days?"

"Sure, Shane," she said with sadness.

After a brief pause, she added, "Well, I guess I had better head back to my dorm. I have a test tomorrow that I need to study for."

"Let me walk you back," he said and started to stand.

"No, that's okay. I think I just need to be alone right now."

"I'll talk to you in a couple of days," he said, and then offered a sad smile.

"All right." And she returned an equally sad smile.

She looked back only once as she walked away. Shane's head was bowed, his eyes were closed. *That's the last time I will ever talk to Shane Robbins,* she thought. Tears began to trickle down both cheeks as she walked slowly back to Bethany Hall.

Chapter 12

Shane continued sitting on the park bench for a long time. *Lord, did I hear you wrong? I have been so sure that You wanted me to pursue Tricia. Did I get my desires mixed up with Yours? I just need to hear from You, God.*

Shane began a three-day fast that very hour. To Shane Robbins, fasting was just another spiritual discipline. *In Matthew, Chapter 6, Jesus said, "When you fast don't do as the hypocrites do…" Jesus said* ***when****, as if assuming we would be fasting sometimes,* he often said to his closest friends who questioned him about this often misunderstood "out-dated" discipline. But he wasn't legalistic about it, either. He fasted when God said to fast, and he fasted what God said to fast. Sometimes the fast was food, sometimes television or a favorite hobby. Sometimes the fast was for a couple of hours, sometimes for a couple of days. This time was different. He had never felt the need to fast and seek God's will as much as he did now. So, for the first time, he committed to a three-day food fast. Three days with no food, just liquids. Mostly water, but sometimes tea or milk. The outward action was not as important as the inward affect.

He spent the first day angry and hungry. *"I might be pregnant,"* replayed over and over in his mind. The thought of Tricia in the arms of another man was nauseating enough for him to not want to eat. He felt furious with whoever the guy was who put her in this position. He really wanted to hit someone. As the day went on, he also admitted that he felt a little angry with God. To find his heart wrapped up in this situation, well, it seemed like cruel and unusual punishment from God. He prayed constantly throughout the day for God to reveal His perfect will for his life, and prayed that he would faithfully serve Him. He prayed for Tricia, too. *God, help her. Lord, she's Yours. She loves You. Please help her.*

The second day he felt led to pray for new eyes to see the situation. He prayed for eyes to see Tricia as God saw her, and for a heart to love her as God loved her. An amazing thing began to happen. As he thought of Tricia, he thought of light and redemption. He thought of purity. He truly glimpsed what God meant when He said in First Samuel 16:7, "Man looks on the outward appearance, but God looks on the heart." By the close of the day, he realized that despite her past experiences, despite the possibilities of her present and her future, one thing was clear. He saw a heart that was lovely and clean and pure through and through. And he wanted to be near that heart.

The third day was the hardest. He was no longer hungry, but felt weak and distracted. He continued to pray, but realized by now all he wanted was to be with Tricia. It just didn't matter what had been or what could be. He realized he only knew what was right then. Right then, he loved her. As he lay down to sleep that night, he prayed, *"I surrender myself to You, Lord Jesus. Give me ears to hear You and a heart to follow You. Show me the way You have prepared for me… And I will follow. Take away my desires and give me Yours alone, Lord. I surrender myself to You."* With that final prayer, he drifted off to sleep.

OOOOOOO

The light was bright, shining through the trees in the beautiful woods. There was an open space up ahead, which was accentuated by the beam of light. Shane walked quietly, but quickly in the direction of the light. He felt drawn to this spot by an outside force, as if he couldn't have stopped his progression, even if he had wanted to. But he didn't want to stop. He urgently wanted to find and see whatever was up ahead. He had to climb over fallen trees, he got caught on thorn bushes, but still he kept walking with his eyes on the light and the clear spot ahead. When he finally reached the clearing, there was Tricia, sitting on a fallen limb. As he approached, she stood. To his surprise, he saw that she was pregnant, maybe seven or eight months along. She was so beautiful. As he walked closer, he heard a voice in the distance. Where is that voice coming from? Is it from above? Or is it coming from the left or right?—*Wherever it came from it was so clear that it was almost tangible. Not a loud booming sound, not a quiet whisper. Just gentle, peaceful, clear words: This is My will for you.*

ooooooo

Shane opened his eyes and felt rested and peaceful. His fast was over. He was sure that God had heard and spoken. He did not know what the future held. He just knew the next step to take.

Chapter 13

Peggy and Mitch walked slowly toward Jane's office. They were very nervous about their meeting. They were scheduled to meet Carla, the birth mother Jane had been telling them about. This was their official "interview" and they were as anxious as they were the first time.

They walked into the office and Jane rose from the chair behind her desk. A dark haired young lady remained seated on the couch on the south side of the room. She looked up at Peggy and Mitch with dark brown eyes tinged with sadness and fear. She quickly looked down at her hands when the couple looked her way.

The ever-cheerful Jane tried her best to make everyone feel at ease. She introduced them to each other and offered a seat to Mitch and Peggy. Peggy moved toward the other side of the couch, but noticed a slight tensing in Carla's posture. She quickly rerouted herself to the vacant wingback chair next to the identical one Mitch had chosen. The air felt tense and thick with anxiety coming from everyone in the room. Jane pretended not to notice and quickly began their meeting.

"Carla, why don't you tell Peggy and Mitch what you are looking for in adoptive parents," Jane began.

"Uh... Well, I don't really know," she said hesitantly.

"Okay, why don't we start with you, Peggy? Why don't you tell Carla about yourself," Jane prompted.

"Well," Peggy began, "I grew up in Knoxville. I have lived here all my life. Mitch and I met at UT when we were both juniors in college. We are both realtors and share an office downtown, although if I ever have an opportunity to be a mom, I want to stop working and stay home with the baby for a few years." With that last statement, a barely noticeable crack in her voice indicated the emotion that threatened to overtake her. Mitch noticed and quickly came to her rescue.

He cleared his throat and began. "We live on the south side of town. We have a 4-bedroom home. We sure would love to fill one of those bedrooms with a baby." He paused to gauge Carla's reaction to his words. Nothing.

"Uh... well, we are both Christians. We would raise a child in a Christian environment. We are active in our church. We both teach a Bible study once a week," Mitch continued. He felt slightly awkward as if he were talking aloud to someone in a deep sleep.

They got very little out of Carla, except the information that they already knew: She was from North Carolina and had lived in Knoxville for three years. She met the birth father in a bar, and he was now completely out of her life. They did glean other information, not so much from her words, but from her attitude. She barely made any references to the baby, and when she did the reference was with the generic "it," as if the baby were an object that unfortunately must be dealt with.

Mitch and Peggy plastered their best smiles on their faces as they were leaving Jane's office. As soon as the door closed behind them, both smiles faded. They looked at each other, silent communication pouring from both of them, but they dared not say a word until they reached the safety of their car.

As soon as both car doors were closed, with them safely inside, Peggy blurted out, "That was horrible! There is no way that girl will pick us to be the adoptive parents. She just plain didn't like us."

Mitch did not disagree, but instead looked silently forward, both hands on the wheel of the idling car. After a moment, he simply said, "We shall see." They drove in silence all the way home.

ooooooo

Both Mitch and Peggy tried their best to keep busy so the waiting would not overwhelm them. Still, their thoughts continually trailed back to the disastrous meeting with Carla. A week later, they were both at home when the phone rang on Thursday evening. Peggy answered while Mitch read the paper across the room.

"Well, she picked you!" Peggy immediately recognized Jane's voice on the other line.

"What?" Peggy replied in disbelief.

"She picked you! We interviewed several other couples, but she says she wants you and Mitch to adopt her baby," Jane replied joyfully.

"Do you think she is really serious about it? I mean—I don't know—I couldn't read her. Do you really think she will go through with it?" Peggy asked cautiously. Mitch had dropped his paper and was now standing right beside Peggy, trying to understand a one-sided conversation.

"I agree. She is hard to read. I hope that's simply because she's nervous and overwhelmed. As always, I can make no promises. All I can tell you is what she is telling me, and that is she wants you to be the adoptive parents of her baby. Do you think you want to proceed?"

Peggy didn't respond right away. She looked at Mitch, who had inched his way close enough to the headset of the phone to hear Jane's words. He nodded in the affirmative. Peggy smiled hesitantly and nodded back.

"Yes, Jane, we want to proceed," she replied with as much enthusiasm as she could muster.

"Are you sure? Do you want some time to pray about it?"

Peggy looked again at Mitch. He smiled at her with understanding and encouragement.

"No. We have prayed about it all week. We definitely want to proceed."

Chapter 14

Tricia looked out the window from her seat in the Elliot University library. Could it have only been a week since Shane showed up again at her dorm room? She still could hardly believe the godly character in this man who pledged to walk with her into the uncertainty of her future. *Who is he? Is he for real?* she often thought.

She had never experienced the type of unconditional love that flowed out of Shane. And yes, it was love. She could say it now. He had made it clear that is what he felt and her heart had melted with the words. And the love she felt in return… well, she couldn't even describe it. She had never felt this way in her whole life. Shane never really described what happened during his three-day fast. It seemed sort of private, just between him and God. But whatever those days of prayer were like, the fruit of them was her current joy. *Praise You, Jesus, for Your incredible mercy,* she often prayed.

They spent most of their free time together now. Each day, Shane asked the same question: "Did you start?"

And each day the answer was the same: "Not yet."

Her days fluctuated between extreme joy and peace because of her relationship with Shane, and great mental anguish and anxiety over what might be—and as each day passed, of what most likely was. She still couldn't bring herself to find out for sure.

She looked up from the history book she was trying, unsuccessfully, to study, to find Shane standing beside her desk in the library.

"Hey, you!" Shane said with affection.

"Hey! I didn't think I would get to see you until after dinner tonight."

"Well, my class got cancelled. The professor is sick. Hate to admit I am glad." He then held out his hand to her. "Come on. Take a break. Let's walk around campus for a little while."

"Gladly!" Tricia replied with a smile. "You saved me from reading the same page for the tenth time!"

They walked hand in hand out of the library and along the beautiful walkways throughout the campus. They didn't speak right away. They were very comfortable in each other's presence even in silent moments. After a while, Shane cleared his throat as if he had something important to say.

"Tricia, I have been thinking—and praying. I know that you don't want to hear this. But… well, Tricia…" he stopped walking and turned her to face him. "You need to know the truth. Either way, you need to know."

She turned from him and began to walk quickly away. It was the first time she had experienced anger toward him. He walked quickly to catch up with her. He gently grabbed her arm, causing her to stop once again.

"Tricia, just hear me out, okay," he said with frustration evident in his voice.

Then, more gently, he continued. "Look. We can't just keep wondering. We need to know. If you're not pregnant," he quickly looked around and then lowered his voice, now barely over a whisper. "If you're not pregnant, then we don't need to keep worrying that you are. We can then just… well… go on. But if you are pregnant, we need to know that too."

"You mean, because then we won't *just go on*?" She said accusingly.

"No, that's not what I mean!" Now it was Shane who felt anger at her for the first time. "I told you I am here for you. I told you I would walk beside you into whatever unknown that you have to face. Gosh, Tricia, I told you I love you. Don't you even understand what that means?" He paused for just a moment and looked away at the landscaped area to his side.

"It means I'm not going anywhere." He said in a tone barely over a whisper.

"But, Tricia, if you are pregnant, if you are carrying a baby, you need to know. You need to know so that you can take care of the baby."

She looked down at her feet, taking in his words. *A baby,* she thought. *If I am pregnant, I need to take care of the baby. Oh Lord, forgive me! I have only been thinking of myself!* Tears then formed puddles in her eyes and overflowed down her cheeks.

"You're right. We need to know."

OOOOOOO

Shane picked up Tricia in a car he borrowed from a friend. He had made all the arrangements for her. He had found a Christian-based crisis pregnancy center listed in the Yellow Pages. When he saw the advertisement promising "confidential and free pregnancy tests," he picked up the phone and called to make an appointment.

They didn't say much on the drive to the center, but Shane reached over to hold her hand. He knew she was scared. He was scared, too. The radio was tuned to a local, Christian station and as they drove they listened to "Healing Love."

So easy to run, but so impossible to hide
When did my whole world come undone,
How many tears have I cried?

I know You're the hope that I've longed for
I believe You have goodness in store
Come be the Healer of my broken
Come with Your mercy and seal all my loose ends

As they drove, hand in hand, they both silently prayed the words coming from the radio. Tricia closed her eyes and let the tears slip down the sides of her cheeks. She prayed as the music played... *Yes, Jesus, I feel You near me. Don't leave me, Jesus. Hold me, Lord. Help me. I'm so scared. Hold me, Lord.*

Shane found a parking place in the back parking lot. They parked and walked together into the unknown future....

ooooooo

"I'm pregnant?" Tricia asked with tears streaming down her face. Hearing these words was so shocking, even though Tricia had suspected she was pregnant.

"Yes, dear, you are," the kind woman from the center answered.

Tricia just sat there, crying, in a state of shock. *Why am I so surprised? I knew it, but I still can't believe it. God, what am I going to do? Oh, Jesus, help me!*

The kind woman handed her a tissue, and sat, holding her hand, offering compassion, not condemnation. After a few moments of silence, she spoke.

"The young man who brought you here—he's the father?" she asked.

"No! No! He is the sweetest guy ever. He would never have done this to me," Tricia replied more harshly than she had intended. *Oh, God! Shane! What is he going to say? What is he going to do now?*

Chapter 15

Two days later, Shirley and Lloyd were finishing a quiet dinner together when the phone rang.

"I'll get it," Shirley said as she rose quickly to answer the phone.

"Mom?" came the shaking voice from the other line.

"Tricia." At the sound of her daughter's voice, Shirley's heart leapt with joy. Finally! Yet, the silence between them had built a wall of bitterness and anger that couldn't be broken down in one conversation. Thus, Shirley's voice took on an emotionless tone.

"How are you?" Shirley continued in the same strained voice.

"Well—uh—I need to talk to you and Dad. Could you ask him to get on the other line?" Tricia replied. Her heart was pounding so rapidly in her chest, she thought she might pass out. She could hear muffled talk and a chair moving across the floor and feet walking to the other extension. After a few moments, she heard her mother's cautious voice once again.

"We're both here now," Shirley said.

"Okay. Hi, Daddy," Tricia began.

"Hi, baby. What do you need to talk to us about?" Lloyd's voice was softer, more hopeful than Shirley's had been.

"Mom, Dad, I need to tell you something." Tricia's voice shook with emotion and she began to sob.

"What is it, honey?" Lloyd asked with compassion.

"This is the hardest thing that I have ever had to do. I've been dreading this. I know it will change everything." Her sobs continued to increase and she paused to catch her breath. In the silence, her mother spoke.

"Are you pregnant?" she asked accusingly.

"What? Shirley!" Lloyd said in defense.

"Well, are you, Tricia?" Shirley pressed her for an answer. The silence said it all. The sobs confirmed the truth.

"Tricia, answer your mom's question. Are you?" Lloyd asked, near panic evident in his voice.

"Yes, sir. I am." Tricia cried in anguish.

Stunned silence. And then Tricia heard a sound that broke her heart into another million pieces. Her father, her strong, stoic father, wept.

ooooooo

An hour later, Tricia's older sister, April, dropped by for a visit with her parents. April and Tricia were so different, it was hard to believe they were sisters. April had long, dark, curly hair, fair skin, and a pretty smile. She was responsible and studious and a rule follower. She was getting her masters in education at the University of Tennessee, so she often saw her parents. As soon as she walked into the den, she knew something was wrong. Her dad looked different, as if he had been.... Crying? She had never seen her dad cry before.

"What's wrong?" April asked with concern.

"Nothing, honey," Shirley quickly replied.

"Nothing? Look, I'm grown now. You don't have to hide things from me."

Shirley and Lloyd looked at each other, both beginning to cry again.

Shirley wiped her eyes with the ragged tissue that she had been twisting in her hand. "We just got a call from Tricia."

"And? Is she okay?" April asked with impatience.

Shirley paused just a moment to clear her throat. "No, she is not okay. She is pregnant." With that, Shirley's tears fell again and Lloyd looked down as his shoulders shook with emotion. After the few seconds that it took for the truth to register in her brain, April wept along with her parents.

ooooooo

April spent an unsettled night in her childhood room. When she awoke the next morning, she grabbed her old bathrobe and went into the kitchen where she found her parents sitting at the table. Untouched eggs sat on two plates in front of both of them. They looked up as April entered the room and sat down at the table beside them.

"What are you going to do?" April asked, getting right to the point. "Will she come home right away?"

Shirley looked at Lloyd, but both were silent.

After a moment, Shirley replied. "We were just discussing that." She paused again. "We just think that it might be unhealthy for all of us for Tricia to come home during this—um—difficult time."

"Not come home? Well, where would she go?" April asked with surprise.

"Well, I don't know!" Shirley responded sharply. "We've never had to deal with anything like this before—and neither have any of our friends!" she said more forcefully than she had intended. Her bitterness was tangible.

"Look," Shirley continued more softly, "when I was in high school, a girl in my class got pregnant. She was ostracized and talked about so badly—even by her so-called friends. I don't want that to happen to Tricia. We've got to protect her."

"Dad, are you okay with this?" April asked turning her attention to her father.

He paused briefly before answering. Tears, once again, welled up in his blue eyes. He suddenly looked old.

"I—I—I just can't. I can't see her and watch her—*change*. I can't see my Tricia like that. I'm sorry."

Everyone fell silent, lost in impossible thoughts.

"Well, what are you going to do?" April asked, breaking the silence.

"I don't know. I just know she can't be here. She can't

go to church with us. I am an elder, for heaven's sake. Do you know the requirements for being an elder? 'He must manage his own family well and see that his children obey him with proper respect. If anyone does not know how to manage his own family, how can he take care of God's church?' First Timothy 3:4,5. Look it up. I am supposed to keep my household in order. I am supposed to have self-controlled children. Yeah, right." His voice caught in his throat. Again, tears welled up in his eyes, threatening to overflow. He couldn't speak anymore.

There was great heaviness in the silence that followed. Shirley's silence emphasized her agreement with Lloyd. Tricia's living at home was not an option. They would have to come up with another plan.

After a long pause, Shirley said, "I have heard of homes for girls in this situation. Out of town. I will find out. People must not know. This is our private problem. We don't need the gossip and the condemnation. Her failure is our failure. We don't have to live out that failure for the rest of our lives. People must not know." Shirley looked pointedly at April, who silently nodded her head in response.

Shirley rose from her chair, determined to find a solution. *Maybe in the Yellow Pages,* she thought.

April left the house with a heavy heart. She fluctuated back and forth between deep sorrow and compassion for Tricia and extreme anger toward her. *Tricia! How could you? How could you have messed up so many lives all at once?* she thought bitterly and not for the first time. *But she is my little sister. I have to do something to help her, even though I want to strangle her.* April gathered her fragile resolve and headed down the street determined to find a solution everyone could agree upon.

Chapter 16

Peggy sat on the back porch with a cup of coffee and a warm blanket. She loved this time of year with all the leaves changing into various shades of golden yellow, bright orange, rusty red. She had her Bible in hand, though she found it hard to concentrate. It was early October and Carla's baby was due in 2 weeks. *Two weeks... could it be that in two weeks I will actually be a mom?* she thought excitedly. They had a baby bed set up in the former guest room. They had bought diapers, formula, and wipes—but just the bare essentials. They knew better than to go overboard. They had been disappointed four times already. But all looked good—so far.

They never seemed to really click with Carla during their visits, but they had begun to accept that reality and assumed it just must be her personality. Still, it bothered them, especially Peggy. There was just something about Carla that she couldn't put her finger on. *Oh, well! Two weeks from now, I won't have to worry about it,* she thought.

She vaguely heard the phone ring from inside the house. She was tempted to ignore it, but since Carla was so close to delivery, she decided to answer. She ran into the house and caught it just before the answering machine picked up.

"Hello?"

"Peggy? It's Carla," was the response on the other line.

"Carla! Hi! Are you okay?" Peggy asked nervously.

"Yes, I'm fine," Carla paused before continuing. "I, uh, wanted to ask you something."

"Sure, Carla. You can ask me anything," Peggy replied, her heart beginning to beat rapidly.

"I, um… I don't really have any clothes for this, um, season. It's getting colder. I was wondering if you could help with that."

Alarm bells began to go off in Peggy's head. Despite going through this process four different times, none of the other birth mothers had ever asked them for money. "Well, Carla, it is getting cooler, for sure. How much do you think you will need?" Peggy asked.

"Well, I was thinking about 300 dollars," Carla said hesitantly.

"Three hundred, huh?" Peggy was frantically trying to figure out what to do. *How much does it cost to buy maternity clothes? I have never been pregnant, how should I know?* she thought to herself. *But I don't want to make her mad. We did agree to help with the medical expenses; maybe this just fits into that. Warm clothes are important…*

"Um, okay, Carla. I think that would be all right. Do you want me to bring it to you?" Peggy asked.

"Well, I could just meet you at the parking lot of the West Town Mall. Maybe in an hour? Would that be okay?" Carla suddenly sounded sweeter, kinder, and more talkative. *Maybe she has just been nervous after all,* Peggy thought.

"Okay, that will work. I will see you in an hour."

"That's great. Thank you, Peggy." Carla replied, her voice filled with relief.

"You're welcome, Carla. See you in a little while," Peggy replied. *Maybe we are making headway with that girl,* Peggy thought with relief. *But why do I have this bad feeling in the pit of my stomach?*

ooooooo

Two weeks came and went. Peggy talked to Jane every day, it seemed. All was well, as far as any of them could determine. For each day that Carla was overdue, Peggy's anxiety grew. *Lord, please let it be today,* she prayed every morning. Exactly six days after Carla's due date, the phone rang as Peggy and Mitch were watching television early in the evening. Peggy ran to answer, with Mitch close behind.

"Hello?" Peggy said breathlessly.

"Hi, Peggy. It's Jane."

"Jane! Is it time?" she asked with excitement.

"Well, yes. But I just got a call from the hospital. The baby has already been born."

"What? I thought we were going to get to be there?"

"Yes, I thought so, too. They wouldn't give me any

information, and I am going to the hospital now. I thought you would want to meet me there."

"Of course! We can be there in 20 minutes." Peggy said, her heart pounding in her chest.

"Great, see you there."

ooooooo

Mitch and Peggy hurriedly got into the car and headed to the hospital. When they arrived at the maternity ward, they saw Jane standing at the nurses' desk. She seemed upset as she spoke to the nurse. She was pointing to papers in her hand.

"Jane?" Mitch spoke as they walked up beside her.

The look on Jane's face spoke volumes. She looked confused, sad, and angry all at once.

"What's wrong?" Peggy said, panic evident in her voice.

"Let's go sit over here and I will explain what I know," Jane responded, pointing to the group of chairs in the area across the hall.

When they were all seated, Jane looked down at the papers in her hands. She looked as if she might cry. Peggy could already feel the tears stinging her eyes.

"Carla left. Apparently, her mother flew in from North Carolina and checked her out of the hospital. They are gone—with the baby."

"What?" Peggy cried. *Lord, how could You?* she silently prayed. Then she thought, *The three hundred dollars! I gave her the money to run away. What have I done?*

oooοooo

In the following weeks, Peggy found herself falling into a deep, dark pit of depression. Anger, bitterness, and disappointment grew deep roots in her heart. She didn't want to see anyone—especially anyone with children. Even Mitch found it hard to get through to her, even though he was struggling with his own sadness. Both began to think that maybe the time had come to give up the fight. *Maybe it just wasn't meant to be,* Mitch thought. Peggy thought the same, but it only increased her depression.

For several weeks in a row, Peggy convinced Mitch that she just couldn't go to church. They had recently heard that a couple in their church had just successfully adopted a little boy. *How could they?* Peggy thought when she heard the news. *They knew how long we have wanted to adopt. How could they? And how could God?* After a month, Mitch insisted that they must go.

On Sunday morning, Peggy stalled at home, insuring that they would walk in late and have to sit on the back row. *That way, we can slip out right after the service, and I won't have to speak to anyone,* she reasoned. And that is just what they did.

They slipped into the back row, just as the congregation finished the last stanza of the first hymn. They sat on the end, close to the exit. Mitch knew Peggy had planned it that way, but he didn't say anything to her about it. He didn't really want to see people, either. But he knew that the isolation would only make their situation worse. *We are supposed to be the Body of Christ,* he thought. *The Bible says, if one suffers, all suffers with it, if one rejoices, all rejoice with it. We definitely need the support—if only Peggy will let them.*

When the scripture was read, just before the sermon, Mitch thought, *Oh, no! Lord, is this a cruel joke?* It was First Samuel, chapter 1—the story of Hannah. *How could that be the text for today, of all days!* he thought. He glanced over at Peggy to see if she was okay. She looked straight ahead, face pale and taunt. *Lord, help her. Please, Lord, speak to her,* Mitch prayed. Their pastor began his sermon, speaking truth with every word.

He began, *"Longing is a feeling to which we can all relate. For all of us there has been a season of life filled with that desperate, empty feeling in the pit of our stomachs. We went on about life, but there were very few moments when we found rest from the longing. We will look at a woman who dealt with feelings of desperate longing year after year. Her name was Hannah.*

We can label our longings with different names, but the feelings are usually the same. The name of Hannah's longing was 'children.' The source of her longing stemmed from an ugly word that was far-reaching in its repercussions: barrenness. *Today, we refer to it as infertility. Many of you may relate to that source of longing. Honestly, I have not. But I have walked beside friends who have, and have partnered in their burden.*

As I studied the story of Hannah, I realized that it matters not what the source of longing is, the source of fulfillment is always the same—life in Christ. So, as we study the story of one particular woman's longing, I want you to apply the lessons we find in Hannah's story to your own source of longing.

Philippians 4:6, 7 says, 'Don't worry about anything; instead, pray about everything. Tell God what you need, and thank him for all he has done. Then you will experience God's peace, which exceeds anything we can understand. His peace will guard your hearts and minds as you live in Christ Jesus.'

Don't worry about anything. Whatever it is that you have longed for, please realize that even in that, God does not want you to be anxious.

But instead, pray about everything. Nothing is too small to talk to God about. You would laugh about some of the things that I pray about. Remember, if you think it, He knows it. So why not go ahead and talk to Him about it?

Then you will experience God's peace, which exceeds anything we can understand. That is what we really need. Peace in the midst of an impossible situation. Peace despite the reality. That does not mean we live in denial or avoidance of the problem. It means we look to Him, because nothing and no one else can help us. The world offers only momentary distraction. God offers perfect peace. Isaiah 26:3 says, 'You will keep in perfect peace all who trust in you, all whose thoughts are fixed on you!'"

Peggy tried to tune out the sermon. *That may work for some people, but not for me,* she thought bitterly. Their pastor continued on while she made a grocery list in her head. But then something he said caught her attention. He spoke of Hannah's encounter with Eli, the priest, after he discovered her in a desperate, emotional surrender to the Lord.

The pastor continued the sermon with these words, *"Eli was there to see Hannah's surrender, and he was used of God to send Hannah a powerful, prophetic word. The word that God had for Hannah that day was 'Go in Peace.' Totally opposite of what she had been feeling year after year. Peace that passes understanding. And that is really what we all long for, isn't it? We eventually come to a point that we long for peace more than anything else.*

Eli said, 'Go in peace.' There is action in the word 'go.' It's as if God wanted Eli to give Hannah the permission to live. Sometimes our problems and longings are so heavy that they weigh us down and we can't move forward. I have seen people even feel guilty about living joyfully in the midst of their problems. We can live in the midst of our longing or heartache by remembering who God is. 'For he himself is our Peace'—Ephesians 2:14. Peace is not found in a change of circumstances, or even in an answer to prayer. Peace is found in a person, God Himself."

Peggy leaned over to Mitch, and whispered, "I am going to the car. You finish the service."

Mitch looked at her with concern and whispered back, "Want me to go, too?"

"No, it's okay. I need a few minutes to myself," Peggy replied.

Mitch spent the rest of the service praying for the wife he loved so much.

ooooooo

The November wind was cold and damp. Peggy got

into the car, turned on the ignition, and then cranked up the heater in the car. She then began to pray to her Heavenly Father. Just as the heater warmed her body, her own prayer of surrender warmed her frozen heart.

Chapter 17

"Tricia Johnson, you have a phone call!"

She ignored it, and walked quickly down the hallway of her dorm. She knew it was Shane, and she couldn't deal with talking to him right now. It had been two weeks since she confirmed her pregnancy, and she had slowly pulled away from him ever since. *He is just too good for me,* she thought constantly. But it was more than that. She also felt guilty. Not just about her current circumstances, but about her current thoughts of how to deal with it. Her mind traveled back to her recent conversation with Kat.

Tricia had called her collect from a pay phone at the far end of the campus, just days after her trip to the clinic. Kat happily received her call.

"Tricia! Hey! I've missed you, my favorite friend! How is college life?"

Hearing her friend's voice brought tears to her eyes. "It's not so great, Kat," Tricia replied with shaking voice.

"What's wrong, Tricia? You can talk to me about

anything."

The loving tone coming from her dear friend broke the dam of her emotions. Kat waited patiently while Tricia composed herself enough to talk.

"I'm pregnant, Kat." Tricia tearfully said.

Uncharacteristic of Tricia's talkative friend, there were several seconds of complete silence, indicating the shock that Kat felt. Finally, she responded.

"Whoa, girl. I'm so sorry. What are you going to do?"

"Well, I guess I'm going to have a baby."

"You don't have to, you know," Kat said very gently.

Tricia was stunned. Whether it was her Christian upbringing, or Shane's good influence, she didn't know, but she had never even considered what Kat suggested. Tricia quickly dismissed it, but a seed was planted in her mind that kept growing and growing. *You don't have to, you know* replayed over and over in her thoughts. *Could it be that simple?* she wondered.

Her overwhelming circumstances and her current thoughts of abortion were definitely hindering her revived heart. She couldn't read the Bible or pray. She spent her time thinking of how she would actually go about getting an abortion. She found herself once again in a dark pit of despair with her softened heart getting more hardened each day.

ooooooo

"I don't think she is here right now," the chipper voice

on the other end of the phone line said.

"Okay, thanks." Shane replied dejectedly.

It had been three days since he had talked to Tricia. He knew she was running away from him. And he didn't know what to do about it. Shane was not one to chase after a girl. He had never had to. But he was so sure that the Lord had spoken to him, he couldn't just take the hint and go away. He had to keep trying. *Lord, help me. I don't know what to do. Give me wisdom, Lord. And help Tricia, too. Speak to her, let her know You are Emmanuel, God with us. In Jesus' name. Amen.*

Chapter 18

Tricia walked to her mailbox in the Student Union. She looked around, making sure Shane was nowhere to be seen. She still avoided him, though it broke her heart to do so. She missed him terribly, but she just couldn't deal with him and her confusing thoughts.

She was surprised to see a letter in her mailbox. Usually, she only received campus announcements. She didn't recognize the name, but quickly opened it. She read,

Dear Tricia,

My name is Shelly Fowler. I am the counselor you spoke with at the center. I got your address from the form you filled out that day. I did not want to make you uncomfortable by calling, but I wanted you to know that I am here for you if you need to talk. My phone number is (863)555-2505 I am usually home by 5:30 P.M. *each day. I hope to talk to you soon.*

Kind regards,

Shelly Fowler

I'm glad she didn't say what center, Tricia thought, as she stuffed the note into her purse. She looked at her watch. Five forty-five. She went into the cafeteria, hoping to eat early enough to once again avoid an encounter with Shane.

ooooooo

As Tricia walked back to her dorm, she replayed the words of the letter over and over again. She didn't want to call Shelly. She wanted nothing to do with the one who had shared the awful news with her. But a force beyond herself seemed to push her toward the pay phone outside of her dorm. Before she could even stop herself, she was dialing.

"Hello?" Shelly Fowler answered the call.

"Uh, hi. This is Tricia Johnson."

"Hi, Tricia. I am so glad you called." Shelly replied.

Tricia felt relieved that she didn't have to explain who she was. But suddenly, she didn't know what to say. Shelly quickly responded to the awkward silence.

"Do you think we could meet to talk, Tricia?" Shelly asked.

"Um, I don't know. I don't have a car." Tricia replied hesitantly.

"Well, how about meeting at the Elliot library. I am there all the time. I am getting my degree in counseling. It won't seem strange that I am there, or that you are talking to me. No one there knows what my day job is."

"Okay, I guess that would work." Tricia replied.

"Will you be available tonight?" Shelly asked. Once again she heard silence on the other line. "How about meeting me at 8:00 in one of the sound proof rooms on the second floor. I study in there all the time."

"Okay," Tricia replied.

"See you then," Shelly said. As she hung up the phone, she prayed, *Lord, give her the courage to come.*

ooooooo

What am I doing? Tricia thought as she climbed the stairs to the second floor of the library. She looked around to make sure she didn't see anyone she knew. She cautiously looked in the window of each of the soundproof rooms. She found Shelly in the one in the corner. The sight of her familiar face brought a sick feeling to Tricia's stomach. She gathered her courage and opened the door.

"Hey, Tricia! I'm glad you came."

Tricia noticed books and notebooks scattered on the table. She sat in the chair opposite Shelly.

Shelly was experienced enough to know that she would have to be the one to carry the conversation. She got right to the point.

"I was wondering if you had figured out what you were going to do." Shelly said.

"Not really," Tricia replied in a noncommittal fashion.

"Well, I don't really know why, Tricia, but I felt the

Lord wanted me to share my story with you." And Shelly began to share with Tricia a story, which took place many years back. A very painful story, with a very tragic ending.

"And that is why I do what I do, Tricia. I don't want young girls like you to make the same mistake that I did. I have found forgiveness and peace, for sure. But I still have to live with this for the rest of my life. Please don't make the same mistake, Tricia. I promise you will regret it if you do."

Tricia was listening so intently that she didn't realize tears were pooling in her eyes, threatening to overflow. She didn't trust herself to speak, but did manage to say, "Thanks for sharing your story." And she got up and slowly walked back to her dorm.

Chapter 19

Shane waited on the other line, while the chipper girl once again announced to Tricia Johnson that she had a phone call.

"I'm sorry, she must not be here," she answered apologetically.

Shane knew that she recognized his voice from all the previous failed attempts at calling Tricia. He felt slightly embarrassed, but gathered his courage and pressed on.

"Look, will you announce that Shane Robbins wants to talk to Tricia Johnson, and he knows she is there because he just saw her go inside?" Shane replied with frustration.

"Uh, okay," she replied hesitantly.

His face burned with embarrassment and frustration as he heard the girl repeat his message.

A few minutes later, Tricia answered.

"Shane, look, I'm sorry, but…" Tricia began, but was interrupted by Shane's strong voice.

"Meet me outside. I'm at the pay phone by your

dorm." He hung up the phone before she could say another word.

He waited outside the dorm for several minutes, feeling like a fool, wondering if she would come. He looked up and saw the front door of Bethany Hall open. There she was. At first, they just looked at each other. The sight of him quickly melted her resolve to break away from him. She walked closer. He spoke first.

"Tricia, you need me right now, and you know it."

"You're right. I do need you. But you don't need me, or my messy life. It is best for you this way, Shane."

"How do you know what is best for me?" he replied angrily. "I'm grown. I can make my own choices, with God's leading. And I choose you, Tricia. Don't push me away."

The final bits of her icy heart melted, and she slowly began to let him back in.

ooooooo

Shane began to study God's Word more than he ever had before. He was driven by a need for guidance and truth. And truth came to him. He knew that he must share it with Tricia. She knew lots of biblical truth, but she was like a patient learning to walk again after a terrible accident. Shane wanted more than anything to help her.

"I was thinking about this place, Bethany Hall, where you are living," Shane said one evening as they sat on the swing on the porch of her dorm.

"Do you know why it's called Bethany Hall?" he continued. "It's a remembrance of the place, Bethany, in the Bible. That is where Jesus ascended into heaven after He rose from the dead. It is also the area of the Garden of Gethsemane where His difficult mission began with blood, sweat, and tears. Don't you see? He began in the garden asking for the cup to pass from Him, yet He willingly drank of it, so that we could be forgiven. After He conquered sin and death forever, He went back to the area where He said, *Not my will, but Thine,* and He rose up to heaven truly fulfilling His words on the cross, *It Is Finished!* Jesus went full circle, so that through His sacrifice He could bring us full circle, too. Tricia, this is not the end of the story. He will redeem this. He will bring this situation and you and me, full circle. It's what He does."

Tricia paused to ponder the truth he was speaking. "But, Shane, you don't need to be messed up by my process of coming full circle. I'm not there, yet. I'm sure God will bring about good through this situation. But I think it will take a long, long time. You don't need to be wrapped up in this, wasting your time and goodness on me."

"Have you ever considered maybe this will bring me full circle, too? Maybe this is His good plan for me."

"How I wish that could be true, but, I just don't know…"

"Tricia, you're going to have to just trust me—and Him. I wish you could have eyes to see yourself as I see you—and even more importantly, to see yourself as He sees you. Then you would know—how much we really do love you." He paused for a moment, wanting to share more with her but wondering if she had heard enough. He decided to continue.

"There was another thing about Bethany," he said.

Tricia smiled a small, teasing smile. "Are you a preacher or something?"

He returned the smile. "No, I'm not preaching, just sharing. There are so many truths that I've been seeing lately. There is just so much I want you to remember about God's love for you. Do you mind?" he smiled and asked hesitantly.

"Of course not. I'm just teasing. Let me warn you, I might be a tough student. I don't seem to learn things the first time very well. But continue, please?" she said with sincerity.

He smiled and said, "Okay. Bethany is also where Jesus let a woman anoint His feet with nard. It was her act of worship, her way of showing Him how much she loved Him. But people didn't understand. You see, nard was very valuable and costly. It was worth a year's wages. It was made with desert grass. You had to be in the desert to gather it." He turned to look at Tricia face to face.

"You are in the desert, Tricia. Start gathering the desert grass and let God turn it into spiritual nard, a thing of value and beauty. And offer it to the Lord. I know you don't feel worthy right now, I know you are worried about what people will think and say. People didn't understand the woman's offering either, and they criticized her for it. Jesus defended her and accepted her offering with great joy. In fact, He said that throughout history, people would talk of her loving act. And they have." He paused to gauge her reaction. When he saw that she was listening intently, he continued.

"You remind me of that woman, Tricia. You remind

me of Mary of Bethany. When you worship—well, I just believe all of heaven rejoices. Especially Jesus. He loves you. He sees you as perfectly pure and cleansed. That is how I see you, too."

"How can you, when you have to see this?" She pulled her t-shirt tight over her belly, showing a slight bump, unnoticeable to anyone else because of Tricia's slender build.

"Because I love you, Tricia. And I understand how this grace thing works. I sin, too. Maybe my sins just don't show as much," he said with a twinkle in his eye. She returned the smile.

"But, what am I going to do? If the school knew, they would kick me out."

"Well, the school doesn't know. No one here knows but me and you, and I'm not telling."

"I can't hide it forever."

"No, you can't. But you can for a while. Even if people notice a change, they will just think it is the 'freshman fifteen,'" he jokingly said.

"Maybe, but this isn't from too much late night pizza."

"I know. But we'll cross that bridge when we get there."

"But Shane, when people find out… they are going to think that it is your baby. Do you understand how that will hurt your reputation? Even if you get a chance to explain, there will always be some people who believe the gossip."

"I know that. It is a risk I'm willing to take, Tricia. I can't control what other people think. You and I know the truth about us. I will only treat you with the respect you deserve,

Tricia. I don't want you to think that I will ever pressure you that way, okay?"

Tricia lowered her eyes and looked at her hands resting in her lap. Shame was like the waves on the beach washing over her time and time again. "I don't deserve respect, Shane," she replied.

"Everyone deserves respect, Tricia." Shane said as he reached over to hold her.

Lord, who is this guy? She thought once again. *Make me worthy of him, and worthy of You. Wash me white as snow.*

Thoughts of abortion never entered her mind again.

Chapter 20

April parked in the least conspicuous parking place she could find. *Oh Lord, please don't let anyone I know see me,* she prayed. She nervously opened the door to Crossroads Pregnancy Center. She had found the address in the Yellow Pages of the phone book. *Tricia owes me big time,* she thought as she found a seat in the waiting room. Three teenage girls scattered around the room, one with an adult woman, probably her mother, the other two with acne-faced teenage boys. All kept their heads down, careful not to make eye contact with anyone else. Though they were all seemingly in the same predicament, they were all isolated in shame and worry. April, too, kept her head down. She felt slightly ashamed of her embarrassment. She just didn't want anyone to think that she, well.... *I just hope they call my name soon,* she thought.

And soon they did. She was relieved to find herself in a comfortable room with two big club chairs sitting side-by-side facing a window. She looked out the window as she waited for the counselor to enter the room. Outside she saw a beautiful garden, with a fountain in the middle. A bronze statue of Jesus holding a child stood in one corner. The pebble-filled pathway was neat and cleared of weeds and surrounded by lovely evergreen and flowering plants. There appeared to be various stations along the pathway, marked with benches and plaques attached to wooden beams. She was too far away to read the plaques.

"Beautiful, isn't it? It's a great place of comfort and healing." A pleasant voice interrupted April's inspection of the garden.

April looked up to see a 4'11" older lady, with short, white hair and crystal clear blue eyes. This surprised April for some reason. She didn't expect to see a grandmother type counselor.

"My name is Pat Smith," the lady spoke with ease.

"I'm April."

"How can I help you, April?" the lady inquired pleasantly.

"Well, I am here because of my sister," April paused to gauge the response from the lady. She expected to see a look of doubt—*Sister, right.* But instead she saw a face focused on listening.

"My sister, Tricia, is at college in Florida. She's pregnant. I'm not sure how far along, I think around 4 or 5 months. She is coming home for Christmas soon, and well, we need help," she blurted out the last phrase as if she just didn't know how else to say it.

"I see," Pat responded not phased by the revelation that seemed so huge to April.

"Do you think she understands about life? Is there danger that she would consider having an abortion?" Pat continued.

April paused. She couldn't imagine that Tricia would ever consider abortion, but she just didn't know. Tricia had certainly surprised her with her choices before. "I don't think so," she replied. "I think that our biggest concern right now is where she will go when she comes home. My parents… they love Tricia very much. But there has been so much hurt over the past year. They just can't handle her moving back home… in this condition. I just wondered if you know of a place she could go… until the baby comes. And maybe you could talk to Tricia about what to do then," April said, glad to be sharing this burden with someone else.

"Yes, I see. We do have much experience with decisions such as these. Could you excuse me for just a moment?" Pat smiled reassuringly at April.

"Uh, okay, sure," April replied.

Pat left the counseling room, went to her office and closed and locked the door. She got down on her knees beside her desk chair. *Lord,* she prayed, *am I hearing You correctly? Do you want me to take this girl in?* Over her 25 years of counseling troubled young girls, she had often felt led to bring various ones into her home to disciple and minister to them during their difficult season. It had been a while since she had shared her home with a troubled girl. But just recently she had felt that stirring. *Is this the one, Lord?* she continued to pray.

Later, April left the center feeling hopeful for the first time in many weeks.

ooooooo

Thanksgiving came and went. Tricia stayed in the dorm, while everyone else fled home to family celebrations. She ate pizza for her Thanksgiving dinner. She just couldn't go home yet. When she told her parents of her decision to stay in Florida over the short holiday, they seemed relieved, though they tried hard to hide it. Tricia understood. She had made their life so difficult for so long.

Though Tricia was again thriving in her faith, her relationship with her parents still remained complicated. *Lord, heal my relationship with them. Help them to forgive me for what I have done, and help me to show them how much I have changed,* she often prayed.

ooooooo

The two weeks before Christmas break were very stressful. Tricia had exams to deal with, and she had to let the registrar's office know that she would not be returning for the spring semester. She made up a lame excuse about her sick grandmother. *Lord, forgive me for that lie,* she prayed. Her roommate, Susan, seemed slightly relieved when she told her she wouldn't be returning. *I bet she had already picked out another roommate anyway,* Tricia thought. Lately, she had caught Susan eyeing her suspiciously. Though Tricia's slim build still hid the pregnancy well, she felt sure Susan suspected the truth, and was glad Susan never asked. The only joy in the midst of this difficult time was her relationship with Shane.

"What am I going to do without you, Shane?" Tricia asked one night, while they studied for exams together.

"I'll still be there for you. We will talk every day." Shane replied gently.

"It won't be the same. Look, Shane, I know you don't like it when I bring this up, but—next semester, well, if you want to date other girls, I understand."

"You still don't totally get it, do you? I love you, Tricia.

I'm not going anywhere. And I am going to remind you of that every day until you believe me."

Tricia smiled a sad smile. *We'll see,* she thought.

ooooooo

Tricia's parents drove to Florida to take her home to Knoxville just before Christmas. The loud anger of the trip to Florida months earlier was now replaced with awkward silence. They had offered to bring her home for a few weeks before she moved to her new home, but Tricia wanted to get settled, plus she couldn't bear to continuously see the disappointment in their eyes. They decided she would at least be at home on Christmas Day. She dreaded it.

ooooooo

Tricia walked into the small apartment and was greeted by an older lady with shining eyes. She immediately felt acceptance, and this was a great relief. Pat Smith led her to a tiny, blue room with an old quilt covering the twin bed. Tricia loved it immediately. It felt peaceful, secure. Hope was tangible in this home. And once again, Tricia praised God for His mercies, new every morning.

Chapter 21

The cold months of January and February dragged on long and lonely. Tricia settled into a routine with Pat. Part of the "deal" of their living arrangement was that Tricia would go through a discipleship program with Pat. Each evening they sat together after dinner and read Scripture and discussed its practical application. Tricia then talked to Shane for a while on the phone and went to bed early. The same routine, over and over. And though Tricia grew spiritually as her stomach grew outwardly, she often found herself bored. That is, until Kat started calling daily too. At first they just caught up on the months they had been apart. Tricia tried to share her newfound faith with Kat, but Kat didn't respond much. Soon, Kat invited Tricia to go out with her to see various old friends. Tricia was very reluctant at first, still embarrassed to be seen in maternity clothes. But Kat had always been very persuasive. And Tricia was so bored and lonely.

OOOOOOO

About 10:00 P.M., the phone rang. Pat shook off her sleepy state and reached over to answer it.

"Hello?" she said groggily.

"Oh, Pat. I'm so sorry to wake you. I thought Tricia would answer." Shane replied apologetically.

"That's okay, Shane. I was just dozing on the sofa. Tricia is not home, yet. She is out with Kat."

He paused, an unsettled feeling coldly passing over him.

"Again? That's the third time this week," he said.

"Yes, I guess it is," she replied.

What is this feeling? Shane thought. *Jealousy? I don't think so. Discernment? Maybe.* "Pat, may I ask you a question?"

"Yes, of course you can."

"Is Tricia—okay?" He asked hesitantly.

Pat could sense what he felt. She felt it, too. "I'm not sure, Shane," she replied truthfully.

ooooooo

An hour later, Tricia came quietly into the apartment. She saw Pat still up, sitting on the sofa, with her Bible opened in her lap.

"Oh, Pat. I hope you weren't waiting up for me. I lost track of time."

"No, I was just studying a bit," Pat replied. "But I am glad I'm still up. I wanted to talk to you, Tricia." Tricia sat beside her on the sofa, and Pat immediately smelled a smoky aroma coming from her clothing.

"Tricia, are you all right? You know you can be honest with me. Believe me, I have seen it all in the past 25 years."

Tricia was silent for a moment. She had once again sensed her heart hardening ever so slightly. She truly did not want to go back to that dark place.

"Well, I promise you, I am not doing anything wrong. But the people that I am with—they don't exactly feel the same way I do about some things."

"You realize that is a dangerous spot to be in, don't you?" Pat asked quietly.

Tricia paused once again, trying to decide her defense. In the end, she simply said, "Yes. I know that."

ooooooo

"Hey, Shane! I have missed you!" Tricia spoke excitedly into the phone.

"I've missed you, too." Shane replied. But Tricia could hear something different in his voice.

"What's wrong, Shane?"

"Well, it's just that—you sure have been busy lately. I have a bad feeling, Tricia. I know that sounds like jealousy. I have confessed it to the Lord, but I don't think it is jealousy." He paused to collect his thoughts.

"I don't know how else to say it, except to just say it. Tricia, your old friends will get you into trouble. That is what happened before, remember? I know that may sound judgmental, but it's not. It's wisdom. Right now, you're not in a place where you can bring them up. They will only bring you down." He paused to gauge her reaction to his words.

"But I promise you, Shane, I haven't run into any of my old—dates." She said, shame washing over her again.

"I'm not worried about that. I am worried about your heart, your spirit," he replied, though he was relieved to hear that news.

"Tricia, I have prayed a lot about this. And it breaks my heart to say it this way. But—you either need to break your old ties, or we need to break up," his voice cracked with emotion as the words flowed from his mouth.

"Do you mean that?" Tricia said, tears pooling in her eyes.

"Yes, I am afraid I do."

Chapter 22

Peggy drove around the block one more time. She wanted to make sure they weren't home. She had been carrying the baby gift around in her car for weeks. She had to deliver it—for herself as much as for the new parents. She had definitely come a long way from her time of surrender back in November. However, her wounds were much like a mending broken arm, workable but weak. That is how she felt—able to function, but weak and dependent on the strength of others, especially Mitch. At least she was now letting people back into her life.

When she was confident that the couple from her church were not at home, she pulled into the driveway, left the car running, and opened the back gate. *Where should I put it?* she thought nervously. She did not want to be there when they returned. She was not ready to face them or their adopted little boy. At least delivering a gift was a step in the right direction. She decided on the grill, in case it rained. She placed the gift inside and lowered the top back in place.

She then walked quickly back to her car. As she drove away, she realized that they probably wouldn't find the present until springtime, when grilling season began again. *Well, I'm not going back,* she thought stubbornly.

The next day, Peggy picked up the phone to call the couple. She hoped that she could just leave a message on their answering machine, but no such luck. A female voice answered immediately.

"Hello?"

"Hi, Carolyn. This is Peggy McGill."

"Hi, Peggy!"

"Listen, I dropped by yesterday with a baby gift, but you weren't there. I left it in the grill. Then it occurred to me that this is not exactly grilling season, and it may be months before you found it. I just wanted you to know it was there."

"That is so nice of you. Thank you so much! I'm really glad you called. I've wanted to talk to you for a while now," she paused a moment, just long enough for Peggy to think, *Oh, no. Don't go there. Please, don't go there.* But, of course, she did.

"I know it may have been awkward for you when we went through the adoption process so quickly. I don't want you to think we are insensitive. I mean, we have prayed for you for a long time. But when this opportunity came up, well, we just felt that the Lord was leading us to this particular child." Carolyn finished her explanation and seemed relieved to have gotten that off her chest. Peggy, on the other hand felt just miserable. *How do I respond to that?* she thought. *In a way that gets me off this phone as quickly as possible, that's how!*

"Of course, I understand. We are happy for you," she said. *Well, maybe not happy, but…*

"Oh, and one more thing I wanted to tell you," Carolyn continued.

Will she ever quit? Peggy thought.

"Our adoption situation came about through Crossroads Pregnancy Center. They don't facilitate many private adoptions, but occasionally it works out. I thought you might want to call there. There is a lady named Pat Smith, who I'm sure would be happy to talk to you. I mean, it's worth a try, right?"

"Yes, thanks for the information," Peggy said sweetly, her heart pounding in her chest.

"And thank you for the gift," Carolyn added.

ooooooo

A week later, Peggy picked up the phone and dialed the number for Crossroads Pregnancy Center.

Chapter 23

"Hey, Tricia!" Kat responded to Tricia's phone call.

"Can we go out to dinner tonight, just me and you? I want to talk to you about something." Tricia asked cautiously.

"Sure! What time?" Kat answered.

They both arrived at the restaurant at 6:00. They sat in a booth in a corner and both ordered burgers and fries.

"So, what do you want to talk to me about?" Kat asked.

"Well, I want to talk to you about my faith." Tricia said simply.

"Look, Tricia, we've talked about that before. You know I support you in your beliefs. I haven't tried to pressure you to smoke or drink or do anything that goes against what you believe. But that doesn't mean that I believe the same things."

"I know, Kat. You have been a true friend to me. You never judged me for my failures or my faith. But my faith is so very important to me now. It's who I am. I hate that we don't have that in common."

"Well, to each his own, right?" Kat replied, slightly

uncomfortable with this conversation. She hoped that cliché would be the end of it, but Tricia still pressed.

"Kat, it's like," she paused trying to think of the right words. "Well, it's like if I had found the cure for cancer, and I knew you had cancer, but I didn't share the information with you. I could say that I loved you, that your friendship was dear to me, but if I didn't share the cure, then my words wouldn't mean much, would they?"

"I guess not," Kat replied, now very uncomfortable with this conversation. Kat functioned best with fun. She and Tricia always got along because they had fun together.

"Well, I do believe that I have found the cure—the cure to the human predicament of sin and death. The cure is only found in Jesus, Kat, and what He did when He died on the cross and rose again."

Oh, great, now she's going to tell me all about Jesus, Kat thought with disgust. "Look, Tricia. I'm not comfortable with this conversation. Like I said, you can believe whatever you want to, for all I care. But don't be trying to force it on me. We always have a blast together. Let's just keep our friendship in the fun category. I don't want any more of these serious talks, okay?" Kat said with frustration.

"Well, that's the point, Kat. I'm different than I was a year ago. I can't keep having fun with you—at least not in the way you want to. What I really want is for you just to consider what I am trying to say. Won't you at least give faith in Jesus a try? Keep an open mind about it, like you do with everything else? Won't you go to church with me, just once?" Tricia said, hopefully.

"Are you kidding? I'm young. Maybe I will consider it when I'm older. But this stuff is not for me. Not now. Please leave me alone about it, okay?" Kat looked and sounded very frustrated.

"Okay, Kat, but if you ever want to talk about it, will you please call me?" Tricia asked sincerely.

"Uh, sure," Kat responded sarcastically.

They finished their meal in awkward silence.

ooooooo

Deep sadness and great relief mixed together for a mind full of confusing emotions. Tricia was glad to be beyond the pull of her past life. She could only hope and pray that one day Kat would understand.

Chapter 24

Tricia lay in bed with her headphones covering her ears. The baby was big enough now that Tricia had trouble finding a comfortable position. She lay on her side, with her knees pulled up as tightly as possible, considering her large belly. She felt the baby kick inside of her, a constant reminder that she soon must decide. She, of course, had only two options: keep the baby or give the baby up for adoption. She spent several days thinking through the option of keeping the baby. She dreamed of tiny clothes and the two of them facing the obstacles together with fierce determination. But then, reality would bring her dream crashing down. *I'm eighteen years old, with no degree, no job, and no way to make a living. I don't even know where I will live after the baby is born. I can't be the kind of parent this baby deserves.* That thought made her weep, night after night. She prayed and wept and curled into a fetal position, headphones in place, listening to music that strengthened her soul.

I know You're the hope that I've longed for
I believe You have goodness in store
Come be the Healer of my broken
Come with Your mercy and seal all my loose ends

Yes, Jesus, be the Healer of all the broken pieces of my life. Don't let me make the wrong decision, Lord. Show me the way.

ooooooo

"Pat, are you sure about this?" Tricia asked, hoping Pat might change her mind.

"I'm sure. If you are willing, then I am sure," Pat responded with a twinkle in her eye.

Crossroads Pregnancy Center had been invited to send a representative to a local Christian high school to speak to the students about purity and abstinence. Pat had suggested that Tricia come along and give her testimony. At first, she was excited. A chance to do something good in the midst of all the bad was very appealing. *But, how will the students react to seeing me in this state?* she worried. In the end, she agreed.

Pat began the talk with statistics and facts mingled with truth from God's Word, and then she introduced Tricia.

Tricia's heart pounded and her whole body shook as she walked up on the stage. In just seconds, as she began to share her own prodigal story, she experienced the peace that comes with purpose. Her present physical condition was testimony enough for the students to understand the consequences of sin. But she also explained about God's amazing grace and His redemptive love and forgiveness.

Tricia did not notice that her parents were sitting on the back row until she neared the end of her talk. Both were teary-eyed. But these were not the angry, hurt tears that she had recently witnessed. Instead these were tears of joy. And there was something else that they exuded which Tricia had not seen in ages. They were proud of her.

Another couple was in the audience to hear Tricia's testimony that day—Peggy and Mitch McGill.

Chapter 25

Once again, Peggy and Mitch sat on the couch in Jane's office. The three of them chatted quietly, while they waited. A short while later, Pat Smith walked in first, a teenage girl trailing behind her. *She is so beautiful,* Peggy thought. She noticed the violin in her hand and marveled at the depth and talent of this unusual girl.

Tricia felt awkward with her violin in her hand, but she had just bought a new bow and didn't want to leave it in the car. She had not met the couple when they came to hear her speak at the Christian high school. From all Tricia had heard about them, they would be wonderful parents to raise this child growing within her. They loved Jesus and served Him with their lives. Their story of waiting for a child for so many years moved Tricia greatly. *Yes, these may be the right ones,* she thought.

The five of them conversed easily throughout the interview. Peggy was overwhelmed with Tricia's love for and obedience to the Lord. She seemed to understand sacrificial love better than others her age. *And it's a good thing, because sacrificial love will have to prevail if Tricia is able to give up the baby for adoption,* Peggy thought.

ooooooo

Tricia sat on the couch in Pat's apartment, the long cord of the phone stretching from the kitchen. Every day ended like this, talking to Shane. They grew closer with every phone call, and she could hardly wait for his visit when the spring semester ended. She moved carefully to a more comfortable position, but quickly found that the move did not bring much relief. It would only be a few weeks now, and as her due date quickly approached, she felt both relief and sadness. Her decision had been made. Papers were being drawn up. She couldn't dwell on it for long, for varying emotions swirled around her heart and threatened to overwhelm her.

"How are you feeling about the McGills?" Shane asked.

"I feel great about *them*, but I feel sad in general. I know that this is the best thing for the baby. They will provide what I can't right now. I wish you were here," she replied with a sigh.

"I will be soon," he said.

When they ended their conversation, Tricia made her way back to her tiny, blue bedroom. She knew she wouldn't be able to sleep until she completed the task that weighed so heavily on her heart. She got out pen and paper and began to write. The first letter was to the delivery nurse at the hospital. She wrote:

To Whom It May Concern:

I know that it will be very difficult when my baby is born. I will be giving the baby up for adoption to a wonderful, loving couple. I feel much peace about this. But please don't offer me the chance to hold the baby after the birth. As much as I would love to, I am afraid that if I do, I won't be able to give her up.

Thank you for understanding.

Tricia Johnson

As she finished the letter, she placed it in an envelope and sealed it shut. Then she began another letter. This one was much more difficult to write. There was so much she wanted to say.

When she finished, her face was wet with tears, and her heart was heavy with sadness. She sealed the second letter and placed both safely in her Bible.

Chapter 26

"We had better talk about names, honey," Mitch said cautiously. This always seemed to be a sore subject. Early on, they had kept a running list of names they liked. But with each failed adoption, the idea of picking out a name was simply painful and disappointing. Still, Mitch felt more peaceful about this situation than he ever had, so he carefully broached the subject.

"Okay, I guess we should," Peggy replied with hesitation. But she, too, felt differently this time. *Maybe this is the situation we have waited for, for so long,* she thought.

"What about a boy's name?" Mitch asked, relief filling his heart. He was so glad that they could talk comfortably about this, once again.

"Well, that's easy. We would name a boy after you. We live in the South; you really need a junior, if you live here," she joked.

He smiled and nodded and then asked, "Well, what about a girl?"

"I have been thinking a lot about that. I was reading about Sarah and Abraham the other day. She laughed when she found out she would finally have a baby at such an old age. I can relate. I think it is hilarious that this is finally working out. Which made me think of the name Hilarie. What do you think?" She looked over at Mitch to see the reaction on his face. This would be even more telling than his words.

"I love it!" He said. "What about a middle name?"

"I have thought about that, too. I know this may sound strange. Many people would not understand this. But Mitch, there is a goodness in Tricia that I love so much. What if we named her after Tricia? Hilarie Patricia McGill. That is what I was thinking."

Mitch looked with love on this unbelievable woman to whom he was married. What kind of woman would consider naming her adopted child after the birth mother? Only one who understood redemptive grace. *Thank You, God for Your amazing grace,* he prayed.

ooooooo

Shane and Tricia sat on the couch together. Her legs were lying over his lap and he lovingly rubbed her swollen feet. They were so glad to be back in each other's presence. Already their visit had been well worth his 750 mile drive. She was still so beautiful to him. He loved everything about her. He just prayed that giving up her child would not break her spirit.

Tricia's back had been hurting all day. She just felt, well—bad. She didn't know what labor felt like, and worried that she wouldn't recognize it when it was time. Once again, she glanced at her watch on her wrist. Shane noticed.

"I've seen you do that several times. You supposed to be somewhere or something?" He joked.

"No, just looking," she said unconvincingly.

"Are you having contractions?" he asked nervously.

"I don't know. I don't feel very good. And my back hurts. And I do feel this tightening every few minutes. But how should I know if that's labor? I've never been through this before."

"Well, Pat should be home soon. We'll wait and ask her when she gets here," he replied. *Oh, God, let her get home soon,* he prayed silently.

As soon as Pat returned home it was determined that a trip to the hospital was in order—just to be on the safe side. They were all fully aware that this could be a false alarm, so they decided that Shane stay back at the apartment, while Tricia and Pat made their way to the hospital.

ooooooo

Peggy was trying to occupy her mind with reading a book, when the phone rang. It was Pat calling from the hospital to let her know Tricia was in labor. Peggy's heart pounded with the news.

"Mitch is out playing golf. Should I go track him

down?" Peggy asked as calmly as she could.

"I don't think so," Pat replied. "With this being her first delivery, it could take many hours. Let us find out what the doctor says when he checks her and I will let you know."

"Okay, I will be waiting here at home."

Peggy put the book aside, knowing that there was no way she could read now.

Fifteen minutes later, the phone rang again. Peggy answered it after the first ring.

"Peggy, I think you'd better go find Mitch."

Peggy and Mitch arrived at the hospital an hour later. They asked a nurse to tell Pat that they were in the waiting room. They sat in the uncomfortable chairs and did exactly what they had been doing for the past 18 years. They waited.

Soon after, they saw Pat coming down the hallway towards them. As they stood to greet her, Peggy felt her whole body trembling. *What if she changes her mind?* she thought. A war raged in her thoughts, and fear threatened to overwhelm her. *Lord, please. We've wanted this for so long.*

After the initial greetings, Pat got right to the point. "Well, she is almost seven centimeters and 95 percent effaced. It still could be a while, but this has gone much quicker than we expected."

"How is Tricia holding up?" Peggy asked with sincerity.

"She is a trooper. Tough as nails, and sweet as can be," Pat replied with a smile.

"Should we just wait here then?" Mitch asked.

"There is a chapel down the hallway. Why don't you

wait in there? I will let you know as soon as the baby arrives," Pat replied, pointing in the direction of the chapel.

"A perfect place to wait," Mitch said.

ooooooo

Tricia pushed with every ounce of strength she had left, then laid back on the bed, exhausted. And then she heard it. A tiny cry, which started out small and weak, but quickly grew louder and stronger. "It's a girl," she heard through the fog of exhaustion. Tears fell from the corners of her eyes, dropping to the pillow on which she lay. Pat and the nurse were by her side, but no one seemed to know what to say or how to react. Congratulations were not in order, yet Tricia still felt she had just experienced the greatest accomplishment of her life. Minutes later, Pat left to tell the McGills the good news of their healthy baby girl's arrival. Soon, Tricia found herself alone in the room with a nurse and her newborn baby.

"May I please hold her?" Tricia asked weakly.

"Oh, but I thought…" the nurse hesitated, obviously due to the letter that she had been given.

"I know what I wrote, but please, just for a minute," Tricia asked with longing.

The nurse looked at Tricia, then looked at the beautiful baby girl. "Yes, of course," she replied with compassion.

She placed the baby, Hilarie Patricia McGill, into Tricia's arms wrapped in a white blanket. Tears poured down Tricia's cheeks, but Hilarie was perfectly still.

"I love you," Tricia whispered. "I will always love you." She kissed Hilarie's tiny forehead, and then she handed the baby back to the waiting nurse.

ooooooo

Pat entered the chapel where Mitch and Peggy sat holding hands. Jane had come to the hospital to be with them while they waited, just as she had so many times before. They all three quickly rose when they saw Pat walking down the aisle of the small chapel. She smiled brightly at them and said, "It's a girl!"

Peggy began to shake so fiercely that she had to sit back down on the pew. Mitch joined her and wrapped his arms around her; they both cried. *Such a long journey. Could this be real after all?* After a moment, they looked up at Pat with tear-stained eyes, waiting for the first instructions on how to be parents.

"I'll come back and get you when the baby is in the nursery," Pat informed them. "They will give you a hospital gown to wear, and then you can hold her and try to feed her."

Wow! After so many years, are we really going to hold our baby? Peggy thought in disbelief.

Fifteen minutes later they were doing just that. Peggy continued to weep as she held her longing, now fulfilled.

ooooooo

Dark, billowing clouds grew larger and multiplied rapidly. Rain poured down, soaking everything in sight. A funnel cloud formed in the distance. Peggy looked out the window and realized that the tornado was coming straight toward her. Where is the baby? *she thought frantically.* She was just here, and now she is gone! Where is she?

ooooooo

Peggy awoke with a start, cold sweat pouring from her pores. She listened for rain or wind or thunder. Nothing. Just the steady sound of deep breathing from Mitch at her side. She had tried for hours to sleep and when she finally drifted off, a nightmare, vivid and terrifying, made rest impossible.

And so she began to pray to her Heavenly Father. *Lord, I'm scared. What if Tricia changes her mind before morning? I have only held Hilarie for one hour, and I now know that I couldn't live without her. And yet, I remember Hannah's response when You finally answered her prayers. She gave her child back to You, Lord. And so do I. I give Hilarie back to You. For her whole life, I will dedicate her to You, for Your glory. No matter what storms may come, I surrender her to You. In the Name, and with the help, of Jesus. Amen.*

Chapter 27

Within an hour of Hilarie's birth, Shane arrived at the hospital. He knocked lightly on the door before entering. When he heard the quiet response, "Come in," he gently pushed the door open. He didn't know what to expect. He just knew that he had to be close to Tricia.

One glance told him that she had been crying. His heart hurt knowing what she must be going through.

"Hey, beautiful. Are you okay?" he asked with concern.

"Yes and no," she replied vaguely, but honestly.

"Wanna talk about it?" he asked.

"No, not really," she replied.

By this time, he had reached her bedside. He reached over and squeezed her hand.

"Whenever you want to talk, you know I'm here to listen," he said.

"I know. I think I just need to process it all for awhile," she explained.

"I know you do. Just remember that I'm here for you," he

said with sincerity. His words proved true. He rarely left her side during the 48 hours she was in the hospital.

When time for Tricia's dismissal drew near, a new doctor came into her room abrubtly, without warning.

He looked pointedly at Shane, obviously commanding with piercing eyes for him to leave the room. Shane quickly rose, pausing just long enough to squeeze Tricia's hand.

Tricia watched as the doctor read over the medical chart. Contempt and judgement oozed from him.

"Your doctor is taking care of an emergency so I will dismiss you from the hospital. The first thing we are going to do is get you on birth control pills," he said with disgust.

"Uh, I don't think that will be necessary," Tricia said, anger and shame rising in her spirit, as redness rose up her neck and face.

"Obviously, it *is* necessary. I will write you a prescription now," he said arrogantly.

"I told you, it is unnecessary. I have learned my lesson," she replied, tears beginning to form in the corner of her eyes.

"Sure you have. I doubt *he* has," the doctor said, pointing in the direction that Shane had walked away.

"Look, the baby isn't his. He is a good guy. I tell you, I won't be needing those pills," she said, clearly upset.

"Yeah, okay," he said with a slight mocking smile on his face. He finished signing the dismissal papers, gave instructions for recovery, layed the paperwork on the table beside her bed, and left the room without another word. On top of the stack of papers was a prescription for birth control pills. Tricia picked it up and looked at it for a long moment. She then wadded it up and threw it as far away from her as she could, and lay back on the pillow and wept.

oooOOOO

Two weeks after delivery, Tricia found herself back in her old childhood home. She and her parents had been through a great healing process in the previous months. Forgiveness had taken place on both sides. After they heard Tricia speak at the school, they had offered to let her move back home. Tricia declined, explaining that she believed she was right where God wanted her to be, and that living with Pat had provided a depth of growth she really needed. They all agreed that she stay right there until the end of her pregnancy. They saw her often and were fully supportive of her. Their support continued now, as they walked with her through this difficult time of recovery and grief.

Tricia sat on her old bed and looked around the room, thinking of days gone by. So much had changed. A certain longing filled her, causing ache in her heart and mind. *I wish I were ten years old again. I would be playing the piano, beginning violin lessons, and going to church each time the doors were open. I would eat spaghetti and not worry if it spilled down the front of my shirt, or left a greasy, rust-colored stain on my upper lip. I would play outside in the sprinklers and catch lightning bugs just before the moon came out...* And then she thought of Hilarie.

Lord, may she have all of these innocent, precious moments and more. Don't let her get lost, like I did. Secure her feet to Your path.

Okay, enough, she thought abruptly. *Too much emotion. I gotta get out of here.* She got up quickly from the bed, afraid if she did not, she would fall once again into the deep pit of sorrow. *Where are my tennis shoes?* she thought with frustration. After a futile search in her closet, she finally located her newest pair of canvas Tretorn® tennis shoes under the bed. She quickly put them on, headed out the door and down the street, running nowhere in particular from feelings that she felt helpless to process.

ooooooo

"Mom!" Tricia called from the bathroom. The urgency in her voice brought her mother quickly to the closed door.

"What's wrong?" her mother asked fearfully.

"I think I need help," Tricia said with shaking voice.

A trip to the hospital confirmed that her body was not yet prepared for the haphazard running. That night Tricia talked to Shane, while she was propped up in yet another hospital bed.

"Tricia, what were you thinking, honey?" Shane said. Fear brought an unintended harshness to his voice.

"I just needed to run," Tricia answered, feeling foolish and immature.

"Were you *trying* to hurt yourself?" Shane asked more gently.

"No. I just needed to run."

"Is it the extra weight? You know that will come off soon

enough, and you look great to me," he continued to pry.

"It's not the weight, not really. But it does bother me, only not for the reasons you think. I don't really care how I look right now. But when I see my body, I think of her," She paused as emotion hindered her speech. Shane waited patiently until she could continue.

"It's just so different. I am different. I went through so much, then got to the end of the struggle, and there's—there's nothing, or rather, no one to hold. Going all the way through a pregnancy, with no one to hold in the end, well—it's just really hard," she finished blowing her breath out, as if it would blow the emotion away.

Six weeks later, Tricia sat Indian style on the floor in a back corner of a small bookstore. She flipped through the pages of *The Complete Book of Running* by Jim Fixx. The cover featured Fixx's muscular legs against a red cover. Within minutes of perusal, Tricia knew she had made all the mistakes of a beginning runner: going out too fast and too long, running in the heat of the day, and not drinking enough to hydrate her body. She soaked in the information, as if drinking cool water on a hot day. She needed a project, a new challenge. Now that she had her doctor's approval, running was that new challenge.

ooooooo

Shane picked up the phone and dialed the number of his dear friend.

"Hello?" she answered cheerfully.

"Jessica, this is Shane," he replied.

"Hi, Shane! How is your summer going? And how is Tricia?"

"Summer and Tricia are both good. But, actually, Tricia is why I was calling." He paused, not quite sure how to proceed. "I want to tell you a story. A prodigal story. But it has to be kept confidential. Is that okay?"

"Shane, you have known me for years. I think you know already that you can trust me. Go ahead, I'm all ears."

So it was when fall rolled around, Tricia found herself back at Elliot University with a new roommate, one willing to disciple her daily and love her unconditionally.

Chapter 28

She waited in the foyer of the church, her dad at her side. Her long white gown fit perfectly over her slender, fit body. The flowers that she held were a mixture of white roses, dendrobium orchids, white asters and gardenias. She looked down at her gown once again. Her thoughts traveled back to a conversation several months ago.

"Maybe I should look for a pale pink gown. I have seen those in some of my magazines."

"Pale pink? Why?" he asked, surprised at the thought of this break in tradition.

She looked down at her hands in her lap. She paused before answering.

"Well… I just don't know if I deserve to wear white," she replied quietly.

He put his arms around her before answering.

"You deserve to wear white more than any person I know. White is symbolic of purity. That is what you are, pure and beautiful. White is also symbolic of God's finished work.

We will all wear pure, white robes one day."

"But I am certain that God's not finished with me yet," she said with a smile.

"He's not finished with me, either. He has done a beautiful, amazing work in your life. Wear the white for Him—as a testimony of His cleansing work in your life. " He pulled her even closer as he spoke.

And so it was that she found herself in this place, at this time wearing white, standing comfortably beside her father who loved her and forgave her. "Healing Love" could be heard coming from inside the sanctuary; a testimony of all they had experienced. As the song ended, the music transitioned into "Jesu, Joy of Man's Desiring," and movement could be heard as all rose to their feet. *Thank you, Jesus,* she whispered, as she and her father walked down the aisle.

ooooooo

Shane and Tricia began their life together with a solid foundation, thoroughly tested in the fire of adversity. They had learned the valuable lesson of forgiveness—both receiving and extending—and this would prove to serve them well in the everydayness of the coming years. In some ways, they were years ahead of others, even as they began their life together. Their greatest joy was living each day bringing glory to the One who had brought them together.

In time, God chose to bless them with tiny reminders of their own youth, first a pretty baby girl, then a handsome baby boy. "Joyful" was the best way to describe the days of their birth. But on both days, there was a moment right after each birth when Tricia's mind traveled back in time to the tiny bundle that she had held in her arms so very briefly. She would never, could never, forget her. But peace ruled in Tricia's heart, always reminding her that the decision was right, was His plan. And thus she continued to live life to the fullest.

Chapter 29

Five-year-old Hilarie stood on the stool at her bathroom sink, brushing her teeth. She brushed the bottom row with as much force as her young hand could manage, hoping to loosen her barely moveable tooth. Her mom, Peggy, picked up dirty clothes from the floor, which had been haphazardly dropped when Hilarie exchanged them for her pink night gown. Hilarie rinsed and spit, content that all was well in the fluoride department.

"Tell me again about why I am yours." She stated the request without any hesitation or awkwardness, as she moved toward her white trundle bed.

"What, honey?" Peggy responded, still focusing on straightening the room and turning down the bed.

"Tell me the story again," Hilarie replied, as she climbed into her soft yellow sheets.

Peggy smiled as she began to tell the familiar story. "Well, for a long, long time it was just me and Daddy." Peggy tucked the sheets around her daughter and then lay on top of them beside Hilarie.

"And we loved each other very much. But we had so much love that we wanted a baby to share it with. So we prayed and prayed and we asked Jesus to send us a baby to love," Peggy continued with ease.

"I love Jesus," Hilarie interrupted.

"And Jesus loves you, Hilarie. Jesus knew that we wanted a baby so much that after a long, long time He answered our prayers by sending you."

"What about the part about my birf mother?"

"Well, your birth mom is named Tricia. That is your middle name, too. And she loves Jesus very much. And she loves you very much. But she was very young and she knew that she couldn't give you the kind of home that you needed. So she picked us to be your mom and dad, because she knew that we would love you soooooo much!" With that last statement, she tickled Hilarie's stomach and heard that lovely laughter that always brought her so much joy.

"I like that story," Hilarie said with contentment.

"Me, too, Hilarie. I like it because it's God's story that He is writing just for us." And with that Peggy prayed over her daughter, turned out the light, and whispered thanks to the One who had answered her prayers, which had begun so long ago.

ooooooo

Peggy and Mitch had settled into the life that they had always dreamed of. They adored Hilarie and each new phase and growth spurt brought with it more joy than they could have imagined. Life was not always perfect, but it was right. Peace reigned in their hearts, minds, and home.

Peggy often thought of Tricia. Her mind would wander toward questions such as:

How is she coping with giving up Hilarie?
Did she graduate from college?
Is she working now as a music teacher or worship leader?
Is she married?

For the first two years, Peggy sent her updates and photos of Hilarie by way of Pat. One day, as she was cleaning the house, the phone rang. She barely heard it over the roar of the vacuum cleaner.

"Hello," Peggy answered, out of breath from running to the phone.

"Peggy? This is Pat. Pat Smith," was the response on the other line.

"Hi, Pat! It has been so long since we have spoken. I hope you have received my packages for Tricia."

"Yes, I have. Thank you so much for being so considerate. In fact, that is why I am calling," Pat paused not quite knowing how to word her request.

"Tricia called me recently very upset," Pat continued.

At those words, Peggy's heart began to pound with dread. *What is she about to tell me? Does Tricia want Hilarie back? She can't! She is legally mine!* All of these thoughts passed through Peggy's mind in a millisecond. Pat continued on, unaware of Peggy's distressing thoughts.

"Tricia wanted me to tell you that she loves seeing the pictures of Hilarie and the updates. She will always cherish the ones she has received. But every time she receives one of your packages, it sends her into a tailspin of grief."

Realization swept through Peggy and brought with it relief as well as deep compassion. "I understand," Peggy replied.

"You have been so gracious to try to comfort Tricia with news of Hilarie, but I am afraid she just can't handle it right now. Tricia never doubts that she made the right decision, but it is still difficult at times," Pat explained.

"I totally understand. I won't send any more photos or updates. But will you give Tricia one last message from me?" Peggy asked.

"Of course, I will."

"Tell her—thank you. Thank you so much. Her gift to us is immeasurable and invaluable and I will be grateful my whole life for her unselfishness. Tell her I will always pray for God's best to come her way," Peggy said with tight throat and tears beginning to fill her eyes.

"I will tell her, Peggy," Pat said, her own voice cracking with emotion.

Peggy hung up the phone and wept. These tears were so different from the ones she had shed for eighteen years. These were tears of joy, tears of thankfulness. But they were also tears of compassion. God had given her a supernatural ability to see into other people's struggles and pain. *Maybe that was some of the refinement that God brought through all my years of struggle,* she thought. And then she whispered a simple prayer. *God, bless Tricia. Show her Your mighty plan for her life. Comfort her in her struggle, as You comforted me for so many years. In Jesus' Name, I pray. Amen.*

Chapter 30

Peggy lay on the couch, while six-year-old Hilarie watched a video beside her. Hilarie was focused on the video; Peggy was focused on Hilarie. She still marveled when she saw her child. *My child. It still overwhelms me that she is mine,* she thought with a tired, but content smile.

Once again, she had not had the energy to do anything but lay around. *At least I am spending lots of quality time with Hilarie,* she thought, trying to be positive.

The pain had started a few months prior in her lower abdomen. A strange, cramping sensation at first, that soon spread throughout the middle of her torso, both front and back. And then the pain was quickly followed by great fatigue. She had been to two doctors already, neither of whom could identify the problem. She was scheduled to have exploratory surgery the following week. She tried hard not to think about it. Fear, like a vice-grip, squeezed at her heart. Sometimes the fear seemed to take her breath away. Other times, she could almost convince herself that nothing was really wrong;

that soon the source of the problem would be discovered and eliminated. But that had never been her life's story thus far. She almost expected a long, hard road ahead. She fought the fear the same way that she tackled every other problem in her life—with faith, prayer, and God's Word.

On the night before the surgery, Peggy and Mitch tried to provide as normal an evening as possible for Hilarie's sake. Peggy's fragile emotions were in check until the point of bedtime. She tucked Hilarie into bed, pulling the covers tightly over her. And then came time for bedtime prayers.

"Bless me, Mom," Hilarie said. She looked so small and precious and pure. Saying the Benediction blessing over Hilarie each night before they turned out the light had become their bedtime routine.

Peggy reached down and placed both of her hands on Hilarie's cheeks, cupping them gently. She looked intently at her child and began the familiar words. "May the Lord bless you and keep you, may the Lord make His face shine upon you, and be gracious unto you…" Her voice began to crack with emotion. Even as the words flowed from her mouth, terrifying thoughts flew through her mind. *This could be the last time I tuck her in… Is she old enough to even remember me if something happens to me?* On and on these waves of doubt and fear flowed over her, threatening to drown her faith and courage.

When Hilarie saw the tears pooling in her mother's eyes, and the emotion affecting her ability to speak, she reached up and placed her small, tender hands on Peggy's cheeks, mimicking the motion of her mother. She cupped Peggy's face with gentleness and love. She continued the blessing all by herself, saying the words that she had heard every night for over a year. "May the Lord lift up His countenance upon you, and give… you… peace." She squeezed Peggy's face gently with each of the last three words, just as her mother had modeled for her so many times.

Peggy embraced her child tightly, and then reached up and turned out the light. "I love you, Hilarie."

"I love you, too Mom."

Later, when the house was dark and quiet, Peggy lay in bed listening to the steady sound of Mitch breathing. In times such as these it is the small details of life, usually unnoticed that capture one's attention. The warmth of body heat radiating from Mitch had always felt soothing to Peggy. She couldn't imagine being able to sleep without feeling him by her side. In the darkness, a heaviness descended on Peggy which felt as if it could smother her in an instant. She threw back the covers and began to walk through the dark house, with only the glow of the street lights illuminating her way. She observed each room with attention to detail that she had forgotten after living there for so many years. She looked at each piece of furniture and remembered where it came from. She lovingly looked at family photos scattered around tables and shelves in every room. *How the photos increased once Hilarie entered our lives,* she thought. She reached out and picked up a photo of Hilarie—her latest school day picture. A sob caught in her throat and the fear once again threatened to smother her. *Oh, God, help me. I'm scared, Lord.*

She walked quickly but quietly to Hilarie's room. She spent a long time staring at her beautiful, sleeping daughter. Once again, the fear gripped her heart. She got on her knees on the floor of Hilarie's room. While Hilarie slept, Peggy poured her heart out to her Lord.

Jesus, help me. I'm so afraid. I don't fear death. I don't even fear the process of dying. But I fear never seeing my baby grow up. I fear that I won't be there for all the milestones. I want to see her plays and programs. I want to listen to her recitals. I want to be there when she loses her first tooth and when she has her first date. I want to be the one to send her off to college, and sit proudly down front when she gets married. Please, Jesus. I waited so long for her. Please don't take me away now. Give me time, Lord. Time to teach her more about You. Time to build up her character. Time to show her in a million different ways how much I love her. Please, Jesus.

Tears poured down her cheeks and she struggled to keep her sobs quiet so as not to wake Hilarie. She grabbed the pillow sham on the floor beside the bed and with muffled sound, continued to weep and pray. She lay there for hours prostrate before her God, beside her child. It was if she was in a battle. Hours later, the battle neared the end, and Peggy had won. She won through surrender. She did not surrender to her fear. She surrendered to her God.

Jesus, not my will but Yours. I know that I offered Hilarie to You the night she was born. Just like Hannah, I gave her to You. It is so hard not to take her back. It's a lie for me to think

I could control her or You or this situation. You, God, are the blessed controller of all things. I surrender once again, my whole life, including Hilarie. Help me not to take her back again. I do believe You, when You say You will never leave me or forsake me. You have proven Yourself over and over again. But help me with the unbelief still residing in the corners of my heart. I'm Yours, Lord. No matter what.

ooooooo

Peggy was on her back on the gurney. Her head was covered in a surgical cap, the scratchy sheets tight around her. As they rolled her down the hallway, the bright fluorescent lights hurt her eyes, still burning with tears. She had just left Mitch and was headed to the unknown of the surgical suite. A kind nurse walked by her side pushing the I.V. stand at the same speed with which the orderly pushed the gurney. When they went through the double doors of the surgical suite, the lights were down low, with the exception of a bright light in the center of the room. The orderly parked her gurney directly under the bright light. Machines, both to her left and right made unfamiliar beeps and sounds, which heightened the reality of where she was and what she was doing. A mask was placed over her mouth and nose, and the soothing sound of the nurse's voice came close to her ear.

"I am going to start counting backwards from 100. You will probably be asleep before I get to 90. Count with me as long as you can, okay?"

Peggy shook her head in the affirmative.

"One hundred, ninety-nine, ninety-eight, ninety-seven, ninety-six…"

Peggy wanted to count with her, but she felt so very tired. So instead of counting, she listened and thought of the greatest loves of her earthly life, Mitch and Hilarie. In her mind's eye, she could see them both with such clarity; she felt as if they were right there beside her. And the last thought she had before she drifted off to sleep was of Jesus. *I trust You, Lord,* she prayed as sleep overcame her.

ooooooo

Five hours later, Peggy woke up in the recovery room. Pain gripped her immediately, causing her to cry out. A nurse was quickly at her side, reassuring her, evaluating her, and then injecting her. As the fog of the anesthesia briefly fled, one thing became very clear: she was alive. If she felt the pain of the incision, it meant she was alive. *Thank You, Jesus,* she thought as she drifted back to sleep.

More thanksgiving came as they heard the results of the surgery—benign ovarian epithelia tumor, with *benign* being the key word. She had once again been given the gift of time.

Chapter 31

Peggy sat perfectly still in the pew beside Mitch. Anyone who saw her would think that she was listening intently to the sermon. Her thoughts, however, were miles away. She replayed the bedtime routine that she had with Hilarie over the past month. Each night Peggy tucked in ten-year-old Hilarie, and each night the same thing occured—questions about Tricia. It didn't bother Peggy, but it made her wonder what was going on in that beautiful head of her precious daughter. Most of the questions evolved around Tricia's life now. *Did she get married? Do you think she has children? If she does have children, what are they to me?* Peggy answered the questions as openly and honestly as she could. She simply didn't know very much. It had been years since she had talked to Pat, their common link to Tricia. After the nightly questions, came the prayers. Hilarie prayed for Peggy and Mitch and friends and other family members. But she also prayed for Tricia and any children that she may have. It didn't trouble Peggy, but it did spark her curiosity.

When the sermon ended, Peggy spotted an aquaintance, Mary Hayes. Peggy knew that Mary often volunteered at Crossroads Pregnancy Center, where Pat worked. She made her way to Mary, who kindly greeted her.

"Mary, I have a question for you. Do you still volunteer at Crossroads Pregnancy Center?"

"Yes, I do. It is a great joy to me. I love helping out there," she replied cheerfully.

"Well, I know you know our story. Do you know if Pat still keeps up with Tricia?"

"Yes, Pat mentions her quite often," Mary replied.

"Well, the reason I am asking is because Hilarie has been very inquisitive lately, mostly about Tricia's family life. Every night for the past month, she has prayed for Tricia and any children that she may have. Do you know if she has any children?"

Mary paused for a moment as her hand flew over her mouth. "Peggy, Tricia gave birth to a little girl three weeks ago." Tears filled both of their eyes as they realized the prompting deep in Hilarie's spirit had been from the Lord.

ooooooo

Mitch tied the laces on his New Balance® running shoes, and then walked to the bottom of the stairs to call Hilarie. Sixteen-year-old Hilarie bounded down the stairs in her own pair of New Balance®, ready for their daily run together. They each leaned against opposite walls of the den stretching first the right leg, then the left leg behind them. Then they sat on the den floor facing each other with first one, then the other leg stretched out in front of them. They reached for their toes and pulled each foot forward as far as possible. Then they got up, took a last swig of water from the sink in the kitchen and set out for a five-mile run.

Three years prior, as Hilarie entered her teenage years, Mitch wanted to find something that they could do together, a way they could keep that connection that they had always had. Running was now the connection.

As they headed out the door and began their run, Hilarie said, "Wait a minute," as she a paused to adjust her shoelaces. He had learned the art of waiting in the eighteen-year journey they had traveled waiting for Hilarie. So he waited patiently as he watched her tie the laces in a double knot to avoid a fall, just as he had taught her. Once again, he looked at his daughter with pride. Her medium length, light brown hair was smooth and shiny. Her build was slim and athletic. And her blue eyes shone with light and life. She was strong and gifted and sweet and stubborn all wrapped up together. And her stellar character within complemented the beauty on the outside. He felt very blessed.

Mitch cherished these times with Hilarie. Sometimes they talked; sometimes they just ran, but it was the togetherness of the event that he most enjoyed.

They ran their usual route, to the park and back, and when they arrived at home, they sat on the front porch sipping cool water from the front water hose.

"Dad, can I ask you a question?" Hilarie said.

"Sure, honey," he replied.

"Well, it's about my birth mother," she replied, testing the level of comfort around this topic. Peggy and Mitch had always answered her questions about her adoption with honesty and openness. Still, it had been such a long time since she had asked questions—she wanted to make sure this was still a comfortable topic of conversation.

"Sure, ask anything," he answered with ease.

"Well, do you know where she lives?"

"Last time I heard, she was in the Dallas area. You know she married a guy named Shane Robbins. But I really don't know where she is. It has been a long time since we had any contact with her."

"She was just a little bit older than I am now, wasn't she?" Hilarie asked.

"Yes, just a couple of years older. She was eighteen," he replied.

"I hope she's happy," Hilarie said.

"Me, too, honey. I hope she is very happy. Because the gift that she gave us in you, has made us the happiest couple I know," he said and smiled lovingly at his daughter.

"I love you, Dad."

"I love you, too, Hilarie."

ooooooo

Tricia paused to tie her shoelaces in double knots. She

had stretched and hydrated. She had 4 packets of GU® safety pinned to the wasteband of her black, Nike® shorts for when her energy got low. She jumped up and down a few times, shaking her arms out in the process. She had run many races in the past few years. But this one was special. This one felt like a picture of her life. Twenty-six point two miles. A long, hard road ahead. A challenge that she had never attempted before. But she was as ready as she could be. She had put in her miles. She had done all of the training that her program required including the taper.

She put her earphones in place. Shane had downloaded 40 of her favorite worship songs, knowing that music still moved her and motivated her and gave her strength and courage. She would need that for the long run ahead. What she feared most was "hitting the wall," as seasoned marathoners call it.

The term "hit the wall" is used to describe the moment in a marathon, usually after mile 20 when the runner has depleted his or her store of glycogen, and this results in a dramatic loss of energy. In short, it's when you run out of gas. But it's not just a physical state, it's also a mental state. It's like running at full speed into a brick wall, over and over and over again. Though not inevitable, it is quite common in the grueling challenge of marathons. *Lord, don't let me hit the wall, but if I do, give me strength to keep going,* Tricia prayed.

Then it happened. Around mile 23, Tricia's legs felt like jelly, as if the support that they normally offered would fail her at any moment. It wasn't that she couldn't catch her breath, it was as if she didn't have breath left to catch.

Tricia had read a comment in *Marathon and Beyond* magazine that described her current condition as a collapse of all human systems, body and brain, soul and spirit. As she continued to put one foot in front of the other, she thought of that statement she had read. *No way,* she spoke silently to herself. *My body may fail, but not my spirit, not my soul.* And with that determined thought came a gentle whisper from the One she loved the most, a reminder of a beloved Psalm... *My flesh and my heart may fail, but God is the strength of my heart and my portion forever, Psalm 73:26.* And with that reminder she pressed on.

The race course turned to the right up a slight hill. The uphill stretch caused her legs to cramp, and she thought she might have to stop. As she pressed through the pain, it became bearable. When she reached the crest of the hill, the course turned left, and suddenly in the distance she saw the finish line. The goal for which she had trained for the past nine months was finally in reach. And still, she wondered if she could make it. Though the crowds cheered, she felt alone. And then she saw him. Shane lifted the rope that divided the crowd from the runners. He didn't say a word; he just began to run with her. And his strength renewed hers, just as it had since the day she met him. As she neared the finish line, she heard him say, "This is yours, Tricia. You can do this. You are not a quitter." And he peeled off to the side and watched with great pride as she crossed the finish line.

With tears streaming, hands raised, and whispered

prayers of thanksgiving, she followed the runners before her down the chute to the help and hydration she so desperately needed. A photographer captured the moment with a flash of his camera—a souvenir of her determined perserverance.

Chapter 32

Hilarie pulled into the church parking lot in her light blue '96 Chevy Lumina. She had a love/hate relationship with her car. She was very thankful to have a car to drive, but with only one working window and only AM radio, some days it was a struggle for her to maintain her positive attitude. Today was one of those days. She was late, not because of poor planning, but because the windshield wipers decided to quit just as a summer storm passed through Knoxville. She slammed the door to her car, and hurried inside the church to the meeting, which had already begun. Wearing faded jeans, a t-shirt, flip-flops, and braided braclets, she looked every bit the teenager that she was. She was on the planning committee for the massive youth event that her youth group was sponsoring as an outreach to the community. She slipped into the only available seat at the long folding table, which had been set up in the youth space. Students began throwing out ideas for speakers and promotion and dates. They had just received word that their budget proposal had been approved and all were excited and full of ideas. She looked around the table at the eager faces before her. She loved this group. This felt like home to her—peaceful, comfortable, and inviting. Her mind traveled back in time to her early days in the youth group. Three years prior, she was an awkward early teen, unsure of her place in life. The faces around this table, especially the youth pastor and his wife, had come along beside her and welcomed her in. They saw something in her that she couldn't see at that time. They invested in her and it had paid off. Her passion for the Lord had grown leaps and bounds, and she realized with grateful heart that He had chosen to use this group of people to bring her to new heights in her journey with Him. Conversation around the table switched to a new topic of planning, drawing her back to the present. Hilarie didn't really have an opinion about the speaker or promotions or dates. She cared about the music; so when that topic arose, Hilarie spoke up.

"Uh, I don't really know who we should consider to lead the worship, but I feel strongly that there are certain things that we should look for in that person. I mean, like, they should be excellent in talent, but they should also have the gift of worship. Worship is, like, preparation for entrance into the presence of God. Worship moves people—at least it moves me," She paused momentarily, not wanting to sound too preachy. She noticed that the others were listening intently, and several were nodding their heads in agreement. But suddenly, she was embarrassed to be so vocal. She wrapped her input up quickly, saying, "And I believe worship moves the hand of God. I just think it will be the worship that opens the hearts of those who come so that they can experience God in their lives." She quickly looked down and grabbed the pen in front of her and began to doodle on her notebook.

"I agree with Hilarie," the youth pastor said. "Hilarie, would you mind heading up a search for the right worship leader?"

"Uh, okay. Sure," she replied. *What have I gotten myself into?* she thought.

The months passed quickly as the youth event neared. Speaker, promotional materials, and worship leader were all secured. When the time arrived, youth from all over the surrounding area showed up for the event. Hilarie felt nervous and excited all at once. And she felt something else: she felt full of purpose.

The worship began that night with instrumentals. Drums, keyboard, electric guitar and acoustic guitar all blended together in harmony. The sound heightened and then mixed with vocals from a male and two females. With eyes closed and hands lifted, they sang together with a spirit of worship pouring out their hearts to God, and an amazing thing happened. It was contagious. Teenagers all over the auditorium sang along, opening their hearts to God, and offering the sweet aroma of pure worship. Just as Hilarie said, their worship moved the hand of God and all could feel His presence. When the speaker walked on stage, with his Bible in hand, hearts were prepared to hear God's Word.

Dressed in jeans and a t-shirt, the speaker didn't look

the part of a powerful preacher, but when he began to speak everyone listened with great attention, as if they couldn't move. He opened his Bible and read a scripture verse, which was very familiar to Hilarie, Romans 8:15, NASB. Her parents had made sure she learned it as a little girl.

> *For you have not received a spirit of slavery leading to fear again, but you have received a spirit of adoption as sons by which we cry out, "Abba! Father!"*

The speaker said, *Mother Teresa once said, "It is a poverty to decide that a child must die, so that you may live as you wish." In our society today, teenagers struggle mightily in battles with their parents. Much of this is perfectly natural. But I am here to say that you must remember that someone gave you life. Someone chose to give the gift of life to you, rather than choose what may well have been easier for them. Regardless, if you have good parents or lousy parents, you must remember and be thankful that they gave you life.*

Now, some of you, like myself, may be adopted. You, my friends, should be doubly grateful. You not only had a birth mom who chose to give you life, but you had adoptive parents who chose to give their lives to you. Sacrificial love surrounds you on every side. This is merely a small reflection of the massive sacrificial love displayed by God, who wants to adopt you as His own child. He wants you to call him Abba. Abba *in the Greek translates not just to Father, but to Daddy. The word Daddy conjures up many things, all involving relationship. Don't you see? God wants a close relationship with you. He wants to spend time with you, care for you, lavish His good and wonderful blessings upon you. But you must accept His offer.*

In this scripture we see two opposite spirits that we can choose from, a spirit of slavery and a spirit of adoption. Both of these have corresponding results. A spirit of slavery leads to fear. A spirit of adoption leads to relationship with the Creator of the universe. Which will it be for you? What do you fear? Don't you understand that you can be freed from all fears when you receive a spirit of adoption, because then you have a Heavenly Father you can run to.

I have young children. When stormy weather comes, I can be assured that shortly, I will hear the pitter-patter of little feet coming down the hallway. Soon, I can feel them climb up into our bed, and wiggle themselves down beside me. Then, they sleep peacefully throughout the storm. And why can they sleep? Because they're close to their daddy! God longs to be that for you. He wants you to come to Him when the storms of life hit. He wants to walk with you and help you through everyday life. He offers you a spirit of adoption. Are you ready to be called a child of God?

The sermon continued, but Hilarie didn't hear much more. She felt overwhelmed by the truth she had heard. She totally understood her birth mother had given her life because of sacrificial love. She also acknowledged that her parents had raised her with sacrificial love. And, yes, she knew of the sacrificial love of Jesus. She had been taught about that her whole life. But suddenly, all the pieces fit together. Silently, she prayed, *Abba, Father. Thank You for wanting me to be Yours. I have always seen You, Jesus, as Savior, but tonight, I surrender myself to You. I want to serve You, Lord. Thank You for the life You've given me. Thank You for my parents who chose me. Thank You for my birth mother who gave me life. May I live my life serving and pleasing You. Whatever You want me to do, I will do. Wherever You want me to go, I will go. I am all Yours, Lord. In Jesus' Name. Amen.*

That night was monumental in Hilarie's life. She didn't tell anyone about it until much later, but she was different. And she never wanted to go back.

The night of the youth event was so successful that a small group of teenagers, including Hilarie, began to gather for prayer each week. As they grew in their faith, they continued to develop a heart for reaching up to God and out to others. As she and her friends sought out authentic worship, they discovered an impromptu event, which affectionately became known as The Burn. The Burn was held in a big, old, dilapidated house in the heart of downtown Knoxville. Inside were second-hand sofas and bean bags scattered around. Christian youth flocked there bringing guitars, mandolins, or any other instrument they had, and there they experienced spontaneous, free worship. It was there that the fire of the Holy Spirit was stirred in their hearts, prompting them toward devotion to God and service to others. Thus the name.

As Hilarie surrounded herself with Christian friends, sincere worship, and submitted to the leadership of godly parents, she grew in wisdom, stature, and favor with God and man. Though she didn't know it, God was answering the sincere prayer of her birth mother: Hilarie didn't lose her way, as so many teenagers do, and her feet were securely fastened to His path.

Chapter 33

One Friday night, after a youth event at The Burn, Hilarie invited three of her friends to spend the night. Typical teenagers, they ate loads of junk food and spent hours texting their other friends. They also crowded around Hilarie's computer and caught up on the latest Facebook status entries on her home page. All of the girls had spent much time with Hilarie and knew her story of adoption. In the safety of these friendships, Hilarie confessed that she did often wonder about her birth mother.

"Do you think you look like her?" one of the friends asked.

"Well, I have never seen a picture, but my mom said she had light brown hair like mine."

"Do you know where she lives?" another asked.

"I don't know for sure, but my dad said he thinks she lives in Dallas."

"Do you ever want to meet her?" the third friend asked hesitantly.

Hilarie paused, unsure of whether she wanted to reveal something that she had never admitted to anyone. "Yes, I do want to meet her one day."

"Do you think that would hurt your parents?" the first friend asked, stating what all three wondered.

"I've thought a lot about that. But they have always been so, like, open and honest with me about my adoption. They've answered all the questions I've ever asked and never made me feel bad for asking. They've always spoken kindly about my birth mother. I actually think they really liked her. I know she is a Christian, and I guess that makes all the difference."

She paused realizing that she hadn't really answered their question. "I guess it might be—weird for them, if I ever met her. But, I'm really close to my parents. They know I love them. I mean, they're my parents, and always will be. I think that if I really wanted to meet her, they would support me in that decision."

Then, one of her friends said that which could change everything. "Let's see if she is on Facebook!"

Hilarie and her three friends crowded together around the computer screen. Hilarie couldn't breathe. It wasn't because her friends were pushing in so closely. It was because she could very possibly be on the edge of seeing the person that she had wondered about for so many years. She clicked on the "Search" button at the top of the screen. Her hands shook as she typed in the name, Tricia Robbins. She looked at her friends. Their faces were lit up with anticipation and excitement. They encouraged her to proceed. With a swift click of the mouse, she pressed the tiny magnifying button at the end of the white search box.

Hundreds of Tricia Robbins appeared. They narrowed the search to Dallas, Texas. As they scrolled through the profile photos of all the Tricia Robbins in Dallas, they saw teenage girls and middle school aged girls. They saw older, grandmother type ladies. But there was only one profile picture that looked like someone that would be the same age as her birthmother.

Hilarie stared at the screen. So did her three friends. Everyone was scared to move. The picture before them was of a middle-aged woman with dark hair pulled back tightly, with a very round face and brown eyes. The expression on her face looked rather stern. She looked hard, haggard, and unhappy.

"Maybe it's just a bad picture," one of her friends offered.

"Maybe it's not her," another said.

"Surely, that's not her. My parents said she was beautiful," Hilarie said.

"A lot can change over seventeen years," the third said more practically.

"That can't be her," Hilarie said, and clicked the red X at the top of her screen.

I hope that's not her, Hilarie thought, feeling guilty even as the thought entered her mind.

Chapter 34

Mitch was reading in bed, when Peggy slipped in between the crisp, cool sheets next to him. She picked up her old worn Bible on her bedside table and began to read from Ecclesiastes. One of her favorites in that book of the Bible was chapter 3—

> *There is a time for everything,*
> *and a season for every activity under heaven:*
> *a time to be born and a time to die,*
> *a time to plant and a time to uproot,*
> *a time to kill and a time to heal,*
> *a time to tear down and a time to build,*
> *a time to weep and a time to laugh,*
> *a time to mourn and a time to dance,*
> *a time to scatter stones and a time to gather them,*
> *a time to embrace and a time to refrain…*

She stopped reading after verse 5, and stared straight-ahead, deep in thought. Mitch looked up and saw her far-off look.

"What are you thinking about?" he inquired.

"Oh, um—Has Hilarie asked you any questions about Tricia lately?"

"Yeah. She did. A few weeks back, after we went running," he replied.

"She has been asking me a lot of questions, too." Peggy sighed, once again staring into space.

"Well?"

"Well, what?" Peggy asked.

"Come on, Peggy. Talk to me. What are you thinking?"

"I don't know. Hilarie seems to want to know. We have always taken the approach of answering honestly anything she asked. I just wonder... if it's time," she said hesitantly.

"Time for what?" Mitch asked.

"Time to give her the letter. Remember when she was born? Tricia gave me that letter. She said that one day she hoped that we would give it to her. She said that when it was time, we would know. I just wonder if it's time," she replied, a slight crack of emotion in her voice.

Mitch reached over and pulled her closer to him. When her head rested on his broad chest, he whispered, "Well, if it is time, the Lord will let us know when and how."

ooooooo

Right before Christmas 2008, Peggy, Mitch and Hilarie were together in the den decorating the Christmas tree. The smell of the pine tree and each of the small ornaments brought back so many memories. Of course there were ornaments gathered pre-Hilarie days, mostly from various trips that they had taken. Peggy's favorite ornaments were the ones that depicted the various stages of Hilarie's life. There was the *Baby's First Christmas* ornament Peggy's parents had given her seventeen years ago. There were the dough ornaments that Hilarie made in kindergarten, and the cardboard picture ornaments she made in elementary school. There was the plaque, which read *World's Best Mom*. It hung on the tree by a wire hanger, covered in plastic beads. Peggy loved Christmas time. Others described her as extremely generous. All she knew was that giving gifts gave her joy. As they hung the last of the ornaments, she knew she had a very special gift to give to Hilarie. At first, as she thought of giving this gift she felt a bit melancholy; and even now it was a bittersweet feeling. But she had prayed about it for weeks, and she knew that indeed, it was time.

She excused herself for a moment and went to her closet, where her grandmother's wooden jewelry box sat on a top shelf. She unfolded the step stool that she kept in her closet and climbed on top of it. Even with the step stool, she had to reach up on her tip-toes to retrieve the box. She brushed off the dust on top and lovingly ran her hands over the carved design, remembering her sweet grandmother. She opened the small drawer at the bottom of the box, and pulled out an envelope, slightly yellowed with age. She held the envelope in her hands for a long time, remembering. Tricia had given the letter to Peggy when they went to the hospital to bring Hilarie home. *Where did the time go?* Peggy thought.

Gathering her resolve, she returned to the den and sat down beside Hilarie on the couch.

"I have an early Christmas present for you, Hilarie," she said.

"A new car?" Hilarie joked.

"No, but I think this will mean more to you than even a new car," Peggy replied.

"Whoa. It must be a pretty good present, then."

Without a word, Peggy handed the letter to Hilarie. Hilarie looked at the yellowing envelope. It had her name written across the front in small, flowing script.

"What's this?" Hilarie asked.

"It's from your birth mother. She gave it to me when you were born. I was reading in Ecclesiastes recently... *There is a time for everything, and a season for every activity under heaven...*" she quoted. "I just thought it was time for you to have this."

Hilarie looked at the envelope again, and then looked up at her mother. "Thanks, mom," she said sincerely.

Sensing that Hilarie needed to be alone, she said, "Dad and I are going out to dinner tonight. Can you fix yourself a sandwich?"

"Sure," Hilarie replied, suddenly very distracted.

Peggy reached over and squeezed Hilarie's hand three times, their family code for "I love you." And then she and

Mitch left the house while Hilarie was introduced to her birth mother for the first time.

OOOOOOO

Hilarie heard the door shut, indicating that her parents had left. She slowly opened the envelope, not wanting to tear the paper. She pulled out folded notebook paper; a reminder of how young Tricia had been when she gave birth. Hilarie barely took a breath as she read.

To The Baby…

To my precious child,
This is so very hard to write. God will be my strength. I became pregnant by accident, but by NO means are you an accident to this world. God has such a beautiful plan for your life. You're kicking me as I write this! When I conceived you I was in total sin and rebellion. But Jesus got a hold of my heart and He showed me compassion and love. I could not have an abortion, but I could not keep you. Because I'm a student in college, I don't have the money, time, or anything else to raise you in a precious home like you're in now. I could not be more pleased with your mom and dad. They are precious people who want a baby more than

anything. They promise to love and devote their lives to you. This is the hardest thing I could ever do. I've felt you grow, kick, and move around for nine months in my body—you are going to be a dynamic person. Please know that I love you and I always will, but this is the best thing that could happen for you. God has told me and confirmed to me that this is the right thing for you and me. I look forward more than anything to the day I finally meet you as a grown woman. I pray you're happy, happy, happy. Let Jesus be your first love and let Him be your best friend. From your mother you developed in, to your mother who will raise you.

I love you my precious baby,
Tricia

In the safety of her solitude, Hilarie wept and wondered at who this woman was now. She felt a connection that she did not understand, maybe as much in the fact that they shared a common love for Jesus as anything. But there was more than that. She could never imagine anyone other than Peggy and Mitch McGill being a parent to her, but she could imagine another kind of relationship—something unique and special between two people bound by blood and spirit. And one thing was very clear: She wanted to meet this woman, sooner rather than later.

Chapter 35

At 7:45 A.M., Tricia dropped off her children at school, leaving them with a prayer and a kiss. She drove straight to the office, wanting to catch up on some paperwork before her Bible study group, which began at 10:30 A.M. She pulled into the parking lot of Parkgate Pregnancy Clinic in Tupelo, Mississippi. They had moved to Tupelo three years prior and had enjoyed the small town charm, so different from their experience in Dallas. She still missed the convenience of shopping and restaurants and activities of the city, but Tupelo had just about everything she wanted or needed. The citizens had welcomed them warmly and they had quickly made close friends. They had found a church they loved and had jumped into ministry, both in their church and in their jobs. Shane worked as CEO of Gumtree Counseling Center, a mental health facility for troubled children and adolescents.

Tricia still marveled at her own job. She was the client director of the local crisis pregnancy center. How many times had she had a chance to share her own redemptive story?

Countless. Her heart went out to every woman who came through the doors, desperate and broken and confused. They usually had another emotion in common—shame. Long ago Tricia had adhered to the advice of Isaiah: *Forget the former things; do not dwell on the past. See, I am doing a new thing! Now it springs up; do you not perceive it? I am making a way in the desert and streams in the wasteland.* And, just as Shane had taught her so many years ago, she had gathered desert grass and offered it to the Lord as spiritual nard, the aroma of which was still powerful in her life. Humbly, she acknowledged that God had done an extraordinary work and her clients responded to her story and her love. Tricia raditated life, and those who experienced the life and love which flowed so readily from her were changed. She was available to her clients long after the hours of operation of the clinic. Often, Tricia texted and talked to a dozen girls at a time, counseling them and pouring acceptance and unconditional love into their fragile lives.

Rarely did they "lose" a baby, but there were those times that a client did choose to have an abortion. Tricia always grieved deeply for those losses, not only because of the death of a child, but also because that could have been her. She still cringed whenever she thought of her brief time of confusion. *Thank You, Jesus, for sparing me the lifelong grief of that decision. May You bring complete healing to those who will walk that painful path*, she prayed frequently.

At 10:15, she got back into her Ford Explorer and drove the two miles to her church. As she parked close to the front of the building, her friend, Traci, pulled up right beside her.

"It's your day, you know!" Traci said cheerfully, after their initial greetings.

"My day?" Tricia asked.

"Your prayer day. Today is your day to get prayed over." She replied.

"Perfect timing," Tricia said with a sigh.

"Still feeling bad, aren't you?" Traci asked, though it was more of a statement than a question.

"Yes. I have been fighting this infection for months now. Just makes me feel lousy. Worse part is, I just can't seem to muster the energy to run. You know how much I need to run."

"I know. But we are going to pray about that. I have a feeling that God is going to heal you soon. He is up to something with you, Tricia. I have been prompted to pray for you so much lately. I can't quite put my finger on it, but He's up to something. I just know it." Traci replied with sincerity.

Tricia just smiled and reached over to hug her dear friend.

As they entered the building together, they were greeted by the friends that had so richly blessed Tricia's life. This small group of women took seriously the mandate to pray for one another. Each week, not only did they take prayer requests from the group, but they also took turns praying over one of the members specifically. If it was "your day" the recipient of the prayers sat in the middle, with all the others gathered around, listening to the Holy Spirit to know what to pray for. It was amazing, the power of the prayers of this small band of faithful women. Years ago, a situation such as this would have made Tricia feel very uncomfortable. Shane was the one to teach her to pray aloud. But now, it was like breath to her. She loved to pray with and for others, and she was grateful when others prayed with and for her.

After their study of the story of Esther, they invited Tricia to sit in the middle. She smiled broadly as she sat down. The others then gathered around her, some standing, some kneeling, some holding her hands.

"Is there anything specific that you want us to pray for?" Traci asked.

"Well, I guess the usual: my family, my clients, my marriage, my ministry…And today, I really need healing." Tricia replied.

"And," Tricia continued, "in light of our study of Esther, pray for me to hear God's voice, to follow His lead, to be willing and ready for whatever extraordinary things He has for me."

And so the women prayed, faithfully and fervently. And the gates of heaven opened, and the Spirit came to revive and prepare. Tricia just didn't realize the answer to their prayers would come so quickly.

Just after the prayer time, Tricia's cell phone rang. It was Pat Smith. Pat had stayed in contact with Tricia over the past seventeen years. They remained very close. Pat was in her late 70's now, and was as spunky as ever. She no longer worked at the Crossroads Pregnancy Center, but was now in the ministry of prayer and wise counsel. Tricia often called Pat for encouragement and advice in her life and ministry. Since the other women had moved into the fellowship phase of the morning, Tricia slipped into the other room to take her call.

"Hey, sweet Pat! How are you?"

"I'm great, dear. How are things in Tupelo?" Pat

answered. There was something in her voice that didn't sound quite right, and Tricia was very curious as to the purpose of this call.

"Pat, you sound different. Is everything really okay?" Tricia asked, with concern.

"Yes, dear, everything is great. I do have something to tell you. Something that may be a surprise to you." Pat paused just long enough to gather the right words together. "Well, I guess I will just say it straight out. Your daughter wants to meet you, Tricia."

Tricia froze. *Did I hear her right?* she thought. It took her several seconds to respond. In the meantime, her heart began to pound, and her body began to shake. Tears filled her eyes. She sat down on the floor, unable to stand on her wobbling legs.

"Pat, are you sure? What about her parents? Are they okay with that? Is she rebellious? Is that why she wants to meet me?" Tricia spouted out question after question in rapid succession, not pausing for answers in between.

"Peggy and Mitch are the ones who called. I met with them and Hilarie. She is a wonderful, mature young woman. She loves the Lord Jesus, Tricia. They have raised her well. She wants to meet you and they support her in that."

"Oh, my gosh, Pat. I can't believe it! What do we do now? Of course, I want to meet her. I need to talk to Shane. I don't even know what to do." Tricia said, her voice cracking with emotion.

"Well, not that you're asking, but I have some advice." Pat said.

"Of course, Pat. I always want to hear what you think."

"Make contact in phases. Maybe with email or what's that new thing that all the kids do now?"

"Facebook?" Tricia replied.

"Yes, that's it. My grandkids tell me I need to get on Facebook. Ha! An old lady like me!" Pat said with a laugh.

"Yes, I'm on Facebook. You think I should contact her that way?"

"I think that would work. But talk to Shane first, of course. If for any reason you think that this is not the time, let me know so that I can tell them."

"There is no reason for me to wait, as long as Peggy and Mitch are okay with it."

"They are. I'm praying for you, Tricia. I think God is up to something wonderful."

"Thanks, Pat, I think you might be right. I will call you soon. I love you."

"I love you, too dear."

Tricia sat on the floor and wept. *My daughter wants to meet me! Is this really happening?* she thought in disbelief. She must have sat there for quite a while, because in time Traci came looking for her. When she entered the room and saw Tricia sitting on the floor crying, she came quickly to her side.

"What's wrong? Are you sick? Does something hurt?" She asked with concern.

"No, I'm fine. It's just that I think God is already answering those prayers." With tears streaming down her face, she told her friend about the phone call from Pat.

Tricia and Traci walked back into the room where her other friends were drinking coffee. One look at Tricia's face, and they came hurriedly to her side.

"What's wrong, Tricia?"

"Nothing bad, but something huge has just happened. I think we need to pray again, if that's okay."

"Of course," several of the women said at once.

Tricia sat back down in the chair in the middle. "I have to tell you a story before I can explain. It is a story that some of you may not know. It is a story of God's redemption. And it began seventeen years ago…"

The women listened and wept as Tricia shared her beautiful story of God's grace. And they did more than that. They prayed, once again, faithfully and fervently.

Chapter 36

Tricia and Shane sat at the computer, staring at the screen. There she was—a photo of the daughter Tricia had always longed to know. How easy it had been to locate her on Facebook, once they had the freedom to do so.

The past week was a blur. Tricia had rushed to Shane's office after the prayer time with her friends to tell him the news. He had, as usual, been there to support her in all her varying emotions. Fear, excitement, joy, anxiety all vied for first seat on her emotional rollercoaster. Another emotion rose up, as well. One with which she was all too familiar, but had not experienced in a long time. Shame revisited once again.

"What does she think of me?" Tricia cried one night when shame had pounded on her heart, like an unwelcome visitor demanding entrance.

"Tricia, whatever she thinks of you now is not important. She will get to know you soon, and will see the beautiful person you are," Shane replied with sincerity.

"But, what if she hates me for giving her up?" Tricia asked, as tears flowed down her cheeks.

"I don't think she would want to meet you if she hated you. Besides, Pat told you that she loves the Lord and has a wonderful relationship with her parents. You're worrying about things that don't exist. I think that you're going to have to trust the Lord in this and 'lean not on your own understanding' like it says in Proverbs."

"You're right. It's just really hard not to go back to that—that—place," she responded.

"I know. I don't want you back there, either. But you are going to have to fight it. You are not that girl anymore. You have nothing to fear or be ashamed of anymore. It has been taken away from you, as far as the east is from the west. Remember Psalm 103? *For as high as the heavens are above the earth, so great is His love for those who fear Him; as far as the east is from the west, so far has He removed our transgressions from us.*"

"I know. You're right. I just wish—that I had been different."

"I understand. We all have regrets. But God has redeemed this, Tricia. This could turn out to be one of the best blessings of your life, which you wouldn't have experienced if you had been different. Just know that He is the redeemer. He turns the bad into our good, if we offer it to Him, and you have. Don't try to take it back."

"Okay, but you are going to have to pray me through this. I feel so burdened to talk to her, to tell her the truth. All of it. I don't know why."

"Well, if God wants you to confess everything to her,

do it. But it might come out little by little over time. Might be better that way."

"You're right."

"I know," Shane said with a smile and reached over to hold his wife while she cried.

ooooooo

Back in the present, they looked at photo after photo posted on her Facebook page. She was beautiful. Tricia stared at the screen, unable to take in the truth of what she was doing.

"So, are you ready to send her a message?" Shane asked.

"Yes! I think. I am just so nervous. I don't know what to say," Tricia responded.

"Just start writing. The Lord will give you the words."

"Okay. Here goes," And with that Tricia contacted her daughter for the first time. Her message read:

> *Hello Hilarie! This is Tricia! I am SO excited that I get to talk to you! I cannot believe this day has come! You have been deep in my heart for so long and I have prayed for you for your whole life. If you are okay with me joining your FB as a friend, feel free to message me as much as you feel comfortable. I would love to hear from you and I can't wait to meet you! Please take care and know that I love you to pieces!*
> *Much joy-*
> *Tricia Robbins :)*

When she finished typing, she looked up at Shane, who was reading over her shoulder. He nodded his encouragement. Tricia looked back at the screen, took a deep breath, and pressed "send." She sat staring at the computer for a couple of minutes, but realized that she had no idea whether or not Hilarie was online. *I can't just sit here. I have to do something to get my mind off the wait,* she thought. So she began cleaning an already clean house, with her phone in hand.

ooooooo

Hilarie sat at her computer chatting with several friends on Facebook. She looked up and saw a number 1 in the red box in the top left corner, indicating a message had arrived. She clicked on the box and her eyes landed on a picture of a beautiful woman with hands raised and tears streaming. The number pinned to her shirt indicated that she had just finished the Music City Marathon. And then she saw the name—Tricia Robbins. *Oh, my gosh! There she is!*

Hilarie's heart pounded and a smile reached from ear to ear. As quickly as she could, she clicked on the reply button and began to correspond with the one that she had wondered about her entire life.

Ten minutes later, Tricia heard a beep on her phone, indicating a Facebook notice. She flew back to the computer, calling for Shane as she ran. And there she found a response from Hilarie, with words that she had longed to hear.

> *Well hey! :) Um, heck yes I wanna be your facebook friend! haha. Can I just tell you that you're awesome? Like for real. when I say there are zero hard feelings or anything of that nature, I mean it. I love you and am simply grateful. This is pretty stinkin cool, dude! :) I'm absolutely stoked to meet you, too. Sounds like you are doing awesome, which completely rocks. I mean heck, let's get this whole meeting thing going as soon as we can! haha.*
> *Excited to talk to you more,*
> *Hilarie :)*

Zero hard feelings kept playing over and over again in her mind. Tears stung her eyes. She picked up her cell phone and sent a blanket text to her prayer group. Over the course of the next hour, friend after friend let herself into to Tricia and Shane's house. Some were in pajamas, some still dressed, some had babies on their hips or sleepy toddlers in tow. But none could stay away. They all had come to celebrate and share in Tricia's great joy.

Tricia and Hilarie continued their Facebook friendship each day. They decided a trip to Knoxville for a face to face meeting would take place on March 28. It would be a long three weeks for both of them as they anxiously awaited the day. One thing that pressed on Tricia immediately after her initial contact with Hilarie was the need to contact Mitch and Peggy. She found herself, once again, staring at a computer screen not knowing what to say. Finally, she did what Shane had advised, and she just began to write, trusting that the Lord would give her the right words. She wrote,

> *Dear Mitch and Peggy-*
>
> *There are no words to say how much I love and appreciate you both and I have THE deepest respect for you guys. I have been in awe getting to know Hilarie this past week and cannot believe what an amazing, strong, Believer she is. You guys are doing such an incredible job with her and I cannot express how good God is! I wanted to communicate with you before I meet Hilarie. I want you to know that I want to be so respectful of you guys and all your desires. I am so forever grateful that you all have been so open with her about me. I am so moved with many tears as I think about how incredible you both have been.*
>
> *I don't know how much Pat has told you all about my life throughout the years. My parents had sent me to a Christian college because they saw the rebellion in my life and prayed God could somehow get myattention there. He did! I met my future husband, Shane, who was a strong Believer and really helped lead me back to Christ. When I told him about my previous rebellion and that I was possibly pregnant, he felt God led him to stick with me—another story within itself!*

Then, I stayed with Pat the months leading up to the delivery and God did a deep, deep work of brokeness and repentance in my life that changed me completely and forever! I always felt God led you both into my life and He was there with me throughout the adoption process. It was definately a God thing! Now that I see Hilarie, the joy that is evident in her life, and her strong relationship with Christ, I can see why God had y'all in mind from the beginning! Isn't it incredible?

I am now working as a counselor at Parkgate Pregnancy Clinic in Tupelo, Mississippi. I am amazed that God has turned my shameful past into ministry. Shane has been working in the field of mental health for the past 16 years and serves as CEO of a mental health facility for children and adolescents. But last year he felt God was leading him toward the ministry and he started a distance seminary program through Liberty University and plans to graduate May of next year. We have been married 16 years this May and are blessed with two kids, Morgan (8) and Ethan (6). So I just wanted to tell you guys a little about us!

I am SO looking forward to my visit up there in two weeks! I am planning to drive up Friday and stay with Pat. Hilarie had mentioned a worship service on Friday night and possibly going to church with you guys on Sunday. I am available for whatever you all want to do. Just let me know what you want to plan. Hilarie seems like such a special girl and, of course, I would LOVE to get to know her more. But I want to be sensitive to her and your desires, so do not hesitate to give me any guidance. Thank you so much for this opportunity. Just the little she has written in the messages over Facebook have meant so much to me! Again, I love and respect you both so much and look forward to getting to know you guys as well.

Take care and God bless you both!

Forever Grateful,

Tricia

Tricia didn't have to wait long for a reply. Sent from Peggy's Blackberry was a simple message that brought with it hope and healing.

Dear Tricia,

We adore you and welcome any relationship. We have looked forward to this day and will leave the details up to you and Hilarie. You gave us an amazing gift we can never repay. We truly are proud for her to meet her godly, beautiful birth mom.

Love,

Peggy and Mitch

Chapter 37

Hilarie passed through the den and headed toward the front door. It was time to leave. She paused when she saw her mom sitting on the couch, reading her Bible. *I wonder how she really feels about all this,* Hilarie thought with concern.

"Mom?"

Peggy looked up from her Bible and replied,

"Yeah, honey?"

"Well, I wanted to know… are you really okay with this?"

"Yes, honey, I really am. I love you so much. I'm excited for you. Really." And Peggy flashed a sincere smile toward her beloved daughter. "In fact, I look forward to seeing Tricia myself tomorrow."

"I love you, mom."

"I love you, too, Hilarie."

With that, Hilarie walked out the door, down the steps, and to her car.

Peggy got up off the couch and walked to the front

window. She watched her beautiful daughter drive away. For a long time, Peggy continued to look out the window. The wind was beginning to blow the new spring leaves on the trees outside. Dark clouds were forming in the distances. *Looks like a storm's coming,* Peggy thought.

As the sky got darker and the rain began to fall, Peggy continued to stand and look out the window. Suddenly, she thought of her dream so long ago. She felt a wave of fear pass over her mind and heart. But it didn't take root. Her faith and her prayers drove it quickly away. *Lord,* she prayed, *I remember my vow to You so long ago. I told You I would give Hilarie back to You. I dedicated her to You for Your glory. I won't take her back now. But give me grace and strength to watch her go. And reveal Your glory in her life and mine.*

ooooooo

Tricia paced back and forth in Pat's small apartment. It had brought back so many memories to be back in this place. The tiny, blue bedroom looked much the same as it had seventeen years ago, and hope was still tangible, even more so, now. Tricia fluctuated back and forth between utter excitement and nervous fear. She didn't know what to expect or what she would say.

Tricia looked around the small den. Her mind traveled back in time to a different occasion, but the same location. She could still remember what she wore to her shower. Pat, so thoughtful and kind, had hosted a "Tricia Shower" instead of a baby shower. The staff of the Crossroads Pregnancy Clinic had gathered in this very room, bearing gifts to cheer her. Bath salts, lotion, new books, and journals... each gift was selected with love. To Tricia's great surprise, Peggy also attended the shower, bearing the best gift of all—a small, leather-bound Bible, which Tricia still cherished to this day.

Back in the present, Tricia reached down into her purse, checking once again to see if her gift for Hilarie was still there. Wrapped in brightly colored paper, indicative of the joy in her heart was a small, leather-bound Bible. She had picked it out intentionally as a response to Peggy's gift so long ago.

Where is she? Tricia thought anxiously. Plans had been made for Hilarie to come to Pat's apartment to meet Tricia face to face for the first time. But she was late. With each passing minute, Tricia's heart pounded more forcefully in her chest. *What if she changed her mind?* Tricia thought. *It would be understandable, but how would I deal with the disappointment?*

The sound of Pat's phone ringing startled her. Pat answered and began to give directions.

"Your windshield wipers aren't working?" Tricia heard Pat say. "Why, dear, that's not safe. It's pouring down rain outside," Pat said, stating the obvious. "Why don't you just wait right there, and we will come get you. We can be there in ten minutes." Pat hung up the phone and looked at Tricia. Without a word, Tricia grabbed her purse and was out the door.

ooooooo

"Now, dear, this is your deal. I will drive up next to her car, you hop out, and I will put it in reverse and be on my way," Pat said with the spunk for which she was known. She then reached over and squeezed Tricia's hand. Tricia didn't speak. Her heart was pounding so loudly, she felt sure that Pat could hear it.

As they pulled into the parking lot, they spotted an old, light blue Chevy Lumina, parked in a lonely spot at the far end of the lot—just what they were looking for. The rain poured down in sheets, making it hard to see ahead. They pulled up near the car, headlights facing each other. Tricia involuntarily let out a cry, jumped out of the car, and into the pouring rain. The car door of the Lumina also opened and out jumped a beautiful teenage girl, with shiny, light brown hair, just like Tricia's. Meeting half way in between the two cars, they both ran into to each other's arms. Tears poured down, mixing with the pouring rain, cleansing body, soul, and spirit.

Pat found that she simply could not just "put it in reverse" as she had said. She sat in the car, both hands on the steering wheel and wept as she viewed the most amazing scene of redemption being played out before her.

ooooooo

Tricia and Hilarie embraced a long time, neither caring about the rain. After a while, Tricia got in the passenger side as Hilarie regained the driver's position in her car.

They watched Pat drive off, and then they headed to a restaurant to begin the process of catching up on seventeen years. While both looked like wet rags, neither seemed to care. By the time they finished their long meal and conversation, they were fairly dry.

They mostly talked of the present. Both had rich, full lives that could fill a million volumes. They immediately had the freedom that comes with Christian fellowship. They talked of their common love for the Lord and of being in service to Him. Tricia was in awe of Hilarie's maturity, depth of character, and intimacy with the Lord—and once again was reminded that Hilarie had grown up in the home of God's own choosing. She was just so grateful to now be a part of this incredible person's life.

When they left the restaurant, the rain had stopped and the night showed hints of stars, shining through the clouds. They drove to downtown Knoxville, past businesses and homes, which looked as if they had seen their better days. They parked near a group of cars lining both sides of the street, and got out of the car. They were headed to The Burn. Hilarie had asked Tricia to go with her to the gathering, explaining that the experience and the friends there were an important part of her life, and she wanted to share it with Tricia.

As they walked up the wooden steps, which creaked with old age, Tricia was reminded of parties of another life. She was Hilarie's age when she walked up similar steps in similar dilapidated homes. But once inside, the former things passed quickly away, and she was confronted with beautiful things springing up. No wild partying inside, just fun and fellowship and true freedom.

As they entered, many eyes lit up as they saw Hilarie. They obviously knew who Tricia was, and came running to meet this one they had been privy to. It was a relief that the way had already been paved so that explanation was unnecessary. Tricia felt overwhelmed with gratitude that Hilarie's teenage choices were so very different from her own. *Thank You, Jesus, for answering my prayers for Hilarie in such incredible ways,* she silently prayed.

Though altogether informal, the time came for the event to begin. This consisted of various individuals grabbing whatever instruments they had brought, and beginning to tune and strum. Within minutes, beautiful chords were played in unison, an impromptu warm-up of beautiful worship. Then without a pause in between, the cords formed into a song that was so very familiar to Tricia. They all began to play and sing "Healing Love."

Tears sprang to Tricia's eyes as she joined in singing the song that God had used over and over in her life.

So easy to run, but so impossible to hide
When did my whole world come undone,
how many tears have I cried?

I know You're the hope that I've longed for
I believe You have goodness in store
Come be the Healer of my broken
Come with Your mercy and seal all my loose ends

Who is this God that holds them all in His hands
and says, though you've pierced Me, I heal your pain?
Who is this Friend that says, I love you even now
and picks my weary heart up off the ground?

I'll never understand
Your embrace of sinful man
But as You hold my heart
it sings a song of love to this merciful King

My closest friend and my first love,
so near yet so high and strong above

I know You're the hope that I've longed for
I believe You have goodness in store
Come be the Healer of my broken
Come with Your mercy and seal all my loose ends

Silently she prayed, *Oh, Jesus, You've always held me, even when I pulled away. How could You love me so perfectly? Thank You, Jesus.* She looked over at Hilarie, flesh of her flesh, so like her, yet so different as well. *Thank You, Jesus, Thank You.* And there, in a dilapidated old home, surrounded by strangers who felt like friends, Tricia worshipped God, the Faithful One, with her daughter.

ooooooo

Peggy stood at the front window and looked outside. The rain had ended. The sky was clear and blue. The storm had passed and left in its place the clean, newness of springtime. The trees were beginning to show signs of green leaves. Early bunches of daffodils lined the driveway and irises scattered themselves in random patches around the house. The old was gone, the new had come—in many different forms.

Peggy had wondered how she would feel when this weekend finally arrived. *I guess I have really wondered for seventeen years now,* she thought. But even if she had tried, she couldn't have conjured up any form of fear or anxiety or sadness. Truly, all she felt was joy. Gratefulness overflowed from her heart. It was as if she could feel His holy brushstrokes painting on the canvas of their lives—a masterpiece in the making.

She stood, waiting with anticipation. Not like the waiting of the past, but a new kind of waiting—one with His signature peace, supernaturally imbedded in her soul.

Emotion was threatening to overflow even before she saw the car pull into the driveway. She reacted in a way, which surprised even her. She ran—not away from the approaching car and its passenger, but to it. And before the car even stopped, she was flying out the door.

ooooooo

Tricia pulled into the driveway, butterflies swarming in her stomach, partly with excitement, partly with fear. She and Hilarie had such an incredible reunion the night before, she almost felt as if it were a dream. The whole weekend, thus far, had proved to be surreal. From Pat's apartment, to meeting Hilarie, to their holy time at The Burn, all of it seemed as it were a part of a vivid, lovely dream—something which is familiar, yet foggy. And more key players from her past were about to enter the scene once again. Tricia was on her way to see Peggy and Mitch. The plan was to go to Mitch and Peggy's home to visit for a while, then take Hilarie for the rest of the day. Despite the precious email she had received from them, Tricia still feared that the welcoming response had faded. Her fears were unfounded.

She put the car in park and looked up toward the house. The front door flew open and out came Peggy running toward her car, tears pouring down her cheeks. Tricia's eyes filled with tears, as well. She opened the door just as Peggy reached the car. Peggy knelt in the space between the open door and the car, so that she could see Tricia clearly, face to face.

"Tricia, we have waited for this day for so long. We couldn't be happier for this time. We love you and have always felt that you were our daughter, too," Peggy said through the tears.

"Peggy, thank you. I just didn't know—how—if—well, just thank you," Tricia said through her own tears.

And the two mothers drawn together by their beautiful girl, embraced and cried tears of joy together.

oooooooo

After a wonderful hour with Peggy and Mitch, Tricia and Hilarie got into Tricia's car and headed to the mountains. It was a beautiful day and they planned to drive and talk and hike and talk some more.

As the city faded behind them, the hills of Tennessee burst forth with budding trees sprinkled with green leaves, and the early blooms of Bradford pear trees. Sunshine filled the car with pleasant warmth and light. Tricia and Hilarie continued their talk of likes and dislikes, similarities and differences, but as much as Tricia was enjoying their time together, each passing mile brought a greater heaviness to her heart. The heaviness was not fear or anxiety, although those were both present. The heaviness was the burden of secrets.

No matter the response, Tricia knew she had to share her past with Hilarie. And so she began her story of a happy childhood, and unhappy years of youth. She didn't—couldn't— hold back. She told it all. She told of choices made which she would forever regret. She told of the progression of sin and shame. She told a tale of a heart, once ripe with godly fruit, and how it hardened into fallow ground. She wept so fiercely as she spoke, that she had to pull over into a clearing surrounded by trees to finish her story.

"I am ashamed to admit to you that I do not know who your biological father is," she said through sobs. "I told my friend, Kat, who the possibilities were. She confronted each one. Each one said, "I'm not the father. Tell her to have an abortion." She paused to wipe her eyes with the tissue she had retrieved from her purse.

"And you must know also, I did consider their advice. Each time I counsel with a pregnant woman considering abortion or with a woman dealing with the traumatic affects of having had an abortion, I remember that it could have been me." Tricia stopped speaking, unable to continue through the loud sobs.

Throughout Tricia's time of confession, Hilarie didn't speak. Tears flowed from her eyes, but they were not tears of anger. She felt no judgment or condemnation toward this beautiful woman beside her. She felt only compassion for the burden that Tricia carried.

Hilarie, with maturity far beyond her years, reached over and took both of Tricia's hands. She looked her straight in the eyes, and spoke peace to her birth mother.

"I forgive you. I am saying that for you, not for me. I say that because I think you need to hear it from me. But honestly, Tricia, in my heart, there is nothing to forgive. You gave me life. And you gave me up so that I could have an incredible life. I am only grateful. As for my biological father—well, so what? I don't need to know who he is. I am just overwhelmed with God's grace in bringing you into my life."

Tricia smiled through the tears. Peace that passes understanding once again returned to her heart. After a long embrace, they continued on their journey to find a mountain to climb—together.

Chapter 38

As spring turned to summer and summer turned to fall, Tricia and Hilarie grew in their love for each other. Their bond was hard to describe—sisters or best friends might come close to describing it, but there was more to it than those labels could offer. It was a holy relationship, as if something missing had finally come, bringing joy and completion.

They corresponded by email, Facebook, phone calls, and visits whenever they could. Hilarie traveled to Tupelo to meet Shane and Morgan and Ethan. She quickly bonded with all of them. She found she had gained another family—one that did not in any form take away from the family in which she was raised, but only enhanced it—an extension of God's will for her life.

This could not have been possible, had Mitch and Peggy not surrendered Hilarie to the Lord so long ago. They refused to feel threatened by Hilarie's growing relationship with Tricia. Instead, they chose joy, realizing that God's masterful plan was writing this story. They did not feel they had lost their daughter to another. They simply felt their family had increased to include Tricia, Shane, Morgan, and Ethan. They had, after all, always longed for a large family. God, in His love, had answered their hearts' desire.

As Hilarie began her senior year, she was assigned the wonderful task of being in charge of the chapel program at her school. An idea formed in her mind, which she prayed about for weeks. After a long time, she finally shared this idea with Tricia one night while talking on the phone.

"I have an idea I want to run past you," Hilarie said cautiously.

"Shoot," Tricia said, good-naturedly.

"Well, you know I am on the chapel committee, right?"

"Sure, I know that."

"Well, I wondered if you might want to come to my school to speak at chapel sometime—like, give your testimony or something," Hilarie replied, relieved to share this idea which had rolled around in her mind for so long.

"I would love to!" Tricia replied, feeling honored to be asked.

As the day approached, Hilarie was beaming with excitement. She knew in her heart and her spirit that this was very important. She didn't know if it was just important to her and Tricia or if it would be pivotal in the lives of others, but she felt compelled to make sure it was completely covered in prayer.

As Peggy drove Tricia to the school that morning, Tricia felt renewed by the beauty of the fall leaves which burst forth with red and yellow and orange and brown. Long ago, Tricia's mom had taught her to view the world through the eyes of God, a reflection of life lessons He longs to teach His children. She remembered riding with her mom this time of year, many years prior.

In her mind's eye, she saw herself as a young elementary student, sitting in the backseat, looking out the window. Her mom, Shirley, glanced at her in the rear-view mirror, and saw the reflective look on Tricia's young face.

"You know, Tricia, God can teach us a lot when we look out the window," Shirley said.

"Like what?" Tricia asked.

"Well, for example, look at all those trees," Shirley replied. "What do you think about them?"

"I think they're really pretty," Tricia said.

"I think so, too. All the colors! It's so beautiful!" Shirley paused to gather her thoughts, looking for just the right words for the lesson on her heart. "But do you know what is really happening?" She paused for a response from Tricia.

"No, Ma'am," Tricia replied. Shirley definitely had her attention.

"They are dying. The leaves are most beautiful when they are dying. It is the same way with us, Tricia. We are most beautiful when we are dying to our selfishness, when we see others as more important than ourselves. That is when we are really beautiful."

That life lesson, shared in the simplicity of everyday life, had always stuck with Tricia. Now, as she drove to Hilarie's school, she realized that she must die to self. A part of her still wanted to hide her past. She sometimes wanted to pretend that she had never strayed away from her First Love. But that would be selfish. He had redeemed her. She was very well aware that so many others needed redemption, too. So, she determined she would allow the Redeemer to make her life beautiful by dying to self.

As Peggy pulled into the parking lot of Christian Academy of Knoxville, Tricia gasped. Peggy looked over at her in the passenger seat, with concern.

"What?" Peggy asked.

"I've been here before," Tricia replied.

"I know. You spoke here when you were pregnant with Hilarie," Peggy replied with a smile.

"How did you know that?" Tricia asked with surprise.

"Because Pat invited us. Mitch and I were in the audience that day. That's when we knew that you could be the birth mother that God had selected to answer our prayers."

"I didn't know that. I was only there that one day. I guess I just didn't remember the name of the school. I was so nervous that day. There were more than one hundred kids there," Tricia said.

Peggy smiled, and reached over and patted Tricia's hand. "There are more than 400 now," she said with a smile.

"Four hundred?" Tricia replied. Her heart began to pound in her chest. *Lord, help me,* she prayed.

ooooooo

Tricia sat on the front row in the auditorium. She dared not look behind her at all of the students filing in. After a few moments of chaos, the students settled down as the headmaster opened the service in prayer. Without introduction, the worship team took their places and began to lead the students in sincere worship. Leading the worship team was Hilarie. Two hearts on the front row both filled with pride—Peggy's and Tricia's. Tricia was amazed and overwhelmed as Hilarie strummed the chords on her guitar and sang with a heart and voice both pure and true.

When the time of worship came to an end, Hilarie stayed on the stage, while the rest of the worship team found seats in the audience.

"Many of you know my story. I was given up for adoption by a young woman, who was, at the time, just a year or so older than I am now. She gave me the great gift of life, and selected the most awesome family for me. God in His amazing grace has allowed her to be back in our lives. I want to introduce you to my birth mother, Tricia Robbins." With that introduction, she traded places with Tricia and sat down beside her mom on the front row.

Tricia walked quickly across the stage and toward the microphone, which Hilarie had just left. As she reached for the microphone, it slipped out of her hand. A look of surprise and then panic crossed her face. She looked over at Hilarie who burst out laughing. Tricia could only laugh too. She bent down and picked up the microphone. She definitely captured their attention with her comic relief. This paved the way for an honest, this-is-who-I-am, straight-from-the-heart talk.

When Tricia finished her testimony, students and teachers throughout the auditorium could be seen wiping at the tears from their eyes. The headmaster dismissed the students back to the classroom, but offered to allow any who wanted to speak to Tricia to remain. Dozens of young women, including a few teachers, remained patiently seated as they took turns speaking with Tricia. Many shared their deepest secrets and struggles; many wanted prayer. All needed someone to listen without condemnation. God was present and mighty in that place.

Two hours later, Tricia climbed into the passenger side of Hilarie's car.

"Whew!" Tricia said as she laid her head back on the seat.

"That was awesome!" Hilarie said, beaming. "I know God did a mighty work. Thanks, Tricia, for coming. You rock!"

"Well, I just pray that God does His mighty work and gets all the glory." She paused, still in awe of the response. "I feel like I just ran a marathon," she said.

"Well, you would know," Hilarie responded with a smile. "You know, I've always wanted to do that."

"Run a marathon?" Tricia asked.

"Yeah. One day I will," Hilarie responded.

"What's stopping you from doing it now?" Tricia asked.

"I don't know. Nothing, I guess," Hilarie replied.

"We could do it together," Tricia said timidly.

"Awesome! Let's do it!" And so they did.

Chapter 39

Tricia sent a training plan to Hilarie each week for the next 7 months. They checked in every day about their progress, both in running and in life. As they shared a common goal, accentuated with hard work and commitment, the bond that they shared grew ever stronger.

Six weeks before the marathon, Tricia's weekly email said: *Let's run 45 miles this week with the long run Saturday being 17 miles and a medium mid-week being 8 miles. Then you fill in the other miles when you can for a total of the 45 miles. I will be running, too. Remember that I am praying for you.* ***But those who hope in the LORD will renew their strength. They will soar on wings like eagles; they will run and not grow weary, they will walk and not be faint. Isaiah 40:31***

I love you, girl! Tricia :)

Three weeks before the marathon, they ran 46 miles including an eighteen-mile-long run. And it was now time to register for the race. They had chosen the Music City Marathon in Nashville because Hilarie wanted her first marathon to be the same one Tricia had first chosen. Tricia registered online for both of them. But just before the event, Tricia received a call from one of the race officials. Hilarie's registration met with resistance because she wasn't yet eighteen.

"I'm sorry, at that age, the runner must be accompanied by a parent," the lady on the other line told Tricia.

"Well, I sort of am her parent." The words flew out of Tricia's mouth before she realized what she was saying.

"Explain, please."

"Well, I'm Hilarie's birth mother. About a year ago, we were reunited," Tricia replied.

The lady continued asking questions and was enthralled with the story. Tricia was able to tell the woman of God's amazing grace. The woman was so moved that not only was Hilarie registered, but she also called the Nashville newspaper, *The Tennessean*, and they ran a human-interest story of Tricia and Hilarie. The headline read, *Running Reconnects Birth Mom, Daughter*. Hilarie was quoted as saying, "It's a really hard relationship to describe because it doesn't fall under any of the terminology most people use to describe a relationship. She is my biological mother, but it's not that kind of relationship. My parents are amazing people and I'm so blessed to have them in my life. And all of a sudden I have this other amazing person in my life to confide in, care about and love."

The last week before the marathon, they tapered off to virtually no running except the marathon on Saturday. They met in Nashville on Friday night, excited and eager to run. They woke up the next morning to stormy weather. Dark clouds hovered over the whole city. Once the rain began, it set up residence for the entire day. Unfortunately, due to injury, Tricia could only commit to the half marathon. But Tricia and Hilarie started out together and ran side by side, in the rain, for 13.2 miles.

At the end of the half-marathon, Tricia peeled off the course and Hilarie kept going. And so did the rain. It poured down, causing puddles in the street, and water in her eyes. It rained so hard it was difficult to see more than a few feet ahead. At mile eighteen, Tricia rejoined Hilarie. They ran side by side once again, Tricia encouraging Hilarie, just as Shane had encouraged her. Then the word came. The weather had gotten so bad that race officials had to block off a four-mile loop of the course, causing runners to finish short of the 26.2-mile goal. Hilarie was devastated. All the training. All the hard work. And she wouldn't be able to reach her goal. Tricia peeled off again, with encouraging words and prayer, and promised to meet Hilarie at the finish line.

As Hilarie continued to run, her determination began to waver. Mentally, she had lost her edge. She wasn't even sure if she could make it the 22 miles that she was allowed. *This isn't how it's supposed to go,* she thought. *I am supposed cross the finish line at the LP Field with a beautiful view of downtown Nashville. Somebody's supposed to cover me with a mylar blanket, place a cool medal around my neck and give me plenty of food and drink. Then me, Tricia, and Shane are supposed to enjoy the bands, and bask in the runner's high. This stinks!*

But just as her disappointment tried to override her

will to run, she remembered the verse that Tricia had sent her during the training, "*But those who hope in the LORD will renew their strength. They will soar on wings like eagles; they will run and not grow weary, they will walk and not be faint.*" And so she prayed that verse over and over, her words lining up in rhythm with the pounding of her feet on the pavement. *Lord,* she prayed, *give me Your strength. I can't do this on my own.*

As she continued to struggle through the race, a runner beside her struck up conversation. He kept looking at his Garmin GPS watch, which told not only his time for the race, but also his distance.

"I have worked too hard for this. I am running 26.2 miles today. I don't care where the race ends, I am just going to run until I reach the 26.2 mile distance."

"Can I come, too?" Hilarie asked, sucking in breath with each word.

"Come on," he replied.

They spotted a parking lot around mile 21. They peeled off the course and ran in circles around the parking lot. Round and round they went until the GPS indicated that they only had a mile left to complete a full marathon. They got back on the race course and ran the last mile to the finish line.

Meanwhile, the rain poured down. Tricia and Shane waited at the finish line. Runner after runner finished their "unfinished" marathon. Thunder roared and lightning flashed. Still no Hilarie. They began to worry. She was still out in the storm, and they didn't know where. Race officials began to take down the equipment. *Still* no Hilarie. Then just ahead they barely spotted her through sheets of rain. They began to shout and cheer and encourage her to the finish line. She crossed the line after four hours and forty minutes and fell into Tricia's arms. Once again, the two were reunited in the midst of a storm.

Chapter 40

Tricia felt the warmth of Peggy's shoulder next to hers, as they sat side by side on the crowded row. She leaned up and looked to her right. Seated beside her was Shane, then Morgan, then Ethan. Next to Ethan sat Tricia's parents, next to them sat April, Tricia's older sister. Tricia then looked to the left. There sat Mitch on the other side of Peggy. He looked so proud. It felt like heaven. So many key players of her life seated together, celebrating with great joy and peace.

Behind them, lined up with all of the other graduates was the object of their celebration. Dressed in royal blue and white, the school colors, Hilarie looked down the aisle and saw both of her mothers, side by side. *Unbelievable,* she thought. It still amazed her to see them together, loving each other and loving her. *Only God could have made this happen,* she thought for the millionth time. "Pomp and Circumstance" began to play and the graduating class of 2010 walked slowly down the center aisle. As Hilarie passed the large group of familiar faces, she lovingly thought of how much her family had expanded in the past year. She smiled at each of them, lingering the longest on Mitch and Peggy, and Tricia beside them.

She was seated just in front of them as she waited not-so-patiently for her name to be called.

"Hilarie Patricia McGill, graduating Cum Laude," the headmaster said loudly and clearly. She walked quickly across the stage and received her diploma. The crowded row filled with her family, cheered.

Caps were thrown, tears were shed, and photos were snapped over and over again. When the last pose was taken, everyone drove to Peggy and Mitch's house for a graduation dinner. The dining room table was piled high with all of Hilarie's favorite foods.

Tricia looked about the room. Hilarie was playing with Morgan and Ethan. *My three children, all together again,* she thought.

She looked in the living room to see Mitch and Shane and her dad seated around the room, sharing stories and the camaraderie of male companionship. Her mother helped Peggy in the kitchen. Tricia just stood and watched, overwhelmed by the goodness of God. She then walked to the piano and began to play a familiar tune. It seemed she had known this tune her whole life, but only now did she truly understand it.

Amazing Grace! How sweet the sound!
That saved a wretch like me.
I once was lost, but now am found!
Was blind but now I see!

To her surprise, voices around the house began joining in unison with the music of the piano.

What they couldn't see was that their voices and pure hearts reached the throne of heaven, and the Father smiled.

ooooooo

Much later, after all the dishes were cleared and most of the guests had left, Tricia, Hilarie, and Peggy sat together on the white swing on the front porch of Hilarie's childhood home. Hilarie, sandwiched between her two mothers, reached out and grabbed a hand on each side of her.

"A cord of three strands is not easily broken," Hilarie said quietly.

Both Peggy and Tricia looked at her.

"What, honey?" Peggy asked.

"A cord of three strands is not easily broken," she repeated. "I read that in my Bible this morning, in Ecclesiastes. That's us. The three of us."

Tricia looked at Peggy and both smiled.

And so they sat, three separate strands, woven together by God's amazing grace. To Him be the glory....

Epilogue

In 1974, Peggy McGill began to pray for a baby to hold and love. She prayed for eighteen long years. The mind of God traveled through time, and saw struggle, and sin, and shame, and hardship to come. And He began His marvelous redemption plan.

In 1974, Tricia Johnson was born. Eighteen years later, in 1992, she was in desperate need of redemption.

In 2010, eighteen years after that, God's plan—at least bits and pieces of it—was clear in the eyes of three women.

ooooooo

Tricia and Peggy once again sat on either side of Hilarie. They had both had their separate turns to speak. The congregation sat silently, taking in every word. They often had opportunities to share their story. But they never tired of telling it or hearing it from each other. Hilarie took the microphone and began to speak.

"My name is Hilarie, and mine is a story of God's grace. Our three separate stories combine to create a masterful plan born in the heart of a mighty God. Our story is not so much about a mother's heart, it is about the Father's heart. When you can't see Him moving, He is. When you can't feel Him beside you, He's carrying you. You must trust the loving heart of the Father. I have found Him to be altogether trustworthy."

Authors' Note

A Cord of Three Strands is a true story. It falls in the widely accepted genre of "creative nonfiction." This means though certain dialog or settings may have been altered, the story is by and large, true. In fact, only God could have written such a detailed, amazing story. We are simply the stewards of His story. We pray we have been faithful stewards and that all the glory goes to Him alone.

Certain names, settings, and dates have been changed to protect the privacy of those included in the story. In parts, one character in the story may represent a group of people in real life. But, as often as is the case, truth is better than fiction, and with that in mind, we have largely kept the details of the story, as they were lived out by Tricia, Peggy, and Hilarie.

We want you to know that God is writing your story, too. Let Him have His way in your life, and you will find an intricate, loving plot, written just for you.

We would love to hear from you and pray for you. Let us know your own story. We know it will be a masterpiece.

Trusting in the One Who loves us best,
Sara and Tricia
www.bethelroadpublications.com

A Word from Peggy

My experience in adoption has been a true blessing. I am an unworthy recipient of God's compassion and grace. But then, aren't we all? I do not deserve Hilarie, and I certainly don't deserve the gift of salvation.

I would advise anyone who seeks God's favor in matters of adoption or anything else to draw close to Him personally, and He will draw near to you.

Come near to God and he will come near to you. Wash your hands, you sinners, and purify your hearts, you double-minded.

James 4:8

For so many years of my life, I am sorry to say that I was not faithful in this. I was the stereotypical Christian—baptized as a child in my present church of FBConcord, a member of virtually all the committees as a young adult, a loving wife of a deacon/committee chair, etc., but it was all vanity and pride because it made me feel important and superior.

"Meaningless! Meaningless!"
says the Teacher.
"Utterly meaningless!
Everything is meaningless."
What do people gain from all their labors
at which they toil under the sun?

Ecclesiastes1:2, 3

My involvement with Bible Study Fellowship International (BSF) convicted me of the shallowness and pride of this way of life.

I would also stress the necessity of intercessory prayer. Just as the Holy Spirit prompted Hilarie to pray for Tricia at the exact time that Morgan was born, so He led others to pray continually for me through this walk. I am so grateful to my dear friends Pat Job, Peggy Buchanan, Melissa Frazer, Betsy Speer, Jan Henley, Carol Connor, Jane Williams, and Mary Beth Jones, just to mention a few; to my brother Jim Harless, and my sisters Anita Loupe, Melanie Harless, and Linda Larsen, who kept me laughing through the tears; to Dr. Larry Rodgers, who diligently sought a baby for us; to my colleagues and the parents at Christian Academy of Knoxville, I am honored to work with you and grateful for your support; to Sara Berry, who interviewed me with professionalism, grace, and much empathy; and finally to Tricia, who truly gave me a priceless gift. To God be the glory forever.

A Word from Hilarie

Purpose is a term that is so often thrown around lightly, but is in reality a deep desire in many people, one that often feels unfulfilled or ignored. It is so easy for us to look at our circumstances—whether it is where we came from, where we are currently, or where we are headed—and feel discouraging emotions and think self-condemning thoughts. For most of us, the tendency is to either blame ourselves or to feel shafted and hurt by God.

Regardless of which of these mindsets we individually are more inclined to battle the sequential thoughts of despair, lack of purpose, and insecurity are the same and are detrimental to the trust and peace that the Lord desires for us all to abide in.

This story is about the two most significant women in my life and how in humility and strength they chose to stand on the Word of God, overcoming and collapsing in that trust and peace.

There are two things that I know with much conviction and passion about God, made very evident in this story: He is a God of purpose and a God of restoration. His Word tells us that even in the darkest of nights we are not abandoned, and that though we may be struck down we are not destroyed. His Word tells us that He makes the broken paths straight, and works for the good of those who love Him. His Word tells us that by His stripes we are healed, that His grace is sufficient for us, and that He is our Shepherd in the most confusing moments.

As you read this story and hear testimony of the merciful and powerful hand of God, see His sweet friendship to us. See His jealous heart for His people. See His nearness to the broken-hearted, and His lifting of the downcast. I am overwhelmed and humbled every day as I see all He has done in my life. My heart overflows with gratitude and passion for His heart and ability to restore. As you read, no matter where in life you find yourself, know this: You are on purpose, and you are passionately loved by a God who is more than able to bring restoration to the most broken and desperate of situations.

The two situations in this story that I "come from," were hard, broken, and desperate situations. They were situations that seemed hopeless, but with much grace and much goodness the Lord brought purpose and restoration to all involved, myself included. Once again, I am beyond humbled and blessed to be a part of this story, and I pray that in reading this the Holy Spirit reminds you of His goodness and His love for you. Be renewed and restored, find your place of sweet surrender to Him, and see His goodness—know it in every moment, and exalt our precious Savior with your everything.

I am still confident of this: I will see the goodness of the Lord in the land of the living. Wait for the Lord; be strong and take heart and wait for the Lord.

Psalm 27:13-14

Weeping may last for the night...

But a shout of joy comes in the morning

Psalm 30:5, NASB

Sara W. Berry

Sara W. Berry, author and creator of many Bethel Road products, has been teaching, be it in a classroom setting or church setting, for the past 17 years. Her experience began at Millsaps College in Jackson, Mississippi where she received a Bachelor of Science Degree in Education, as well as numerous education and leadership awards. Her varied work experience includes teaching elementary students in Memphis, TN; Nashville, TN; Jackson, MS; Costa Rica and Ecuador. She was director of a tutorial program for inner city children in Jackson, MS as well as program director for an inner city humanitarian service in Memphis, TN. She also served as children's director for her church.

She is married to Dr. Mont Berry and her teaching experience continues each day as she is rearing her six children: Katie, Ellie, Joseph, Troy, Joshua, and Sara Ruth.

Sara has an intense love for discipleship. She desires to teach, through her books and curriculum, the truth of God's Word, knowing that the Word does not return void. Sara has an equal passion for missions. She has taken seriously the mandate of the Great Commission. She lived in San Jose, Costa Rica as a missionary teacher in the late 1980s. After her marriage to Mont, they both lived in Shell Mera, Ecuador, he working at a jungle hospital, she teaching at the Nate Saint Memorial School. Most recently, the entire Berry family spent time in mission service in Peru and Nicaragua. In recent years, Sara also spent time in China. At present, several of Sara's programs are being translated into Spanish, Chinese and Hindi.

With the gift of teaching, and a passion for discipleship, Sara Berry finds great joy in sharing the truth of the Scriptures with others. Sara has shared her material from *Stones from the River Jordan* with hundreds of women from the United States, South America and China. If you are interested in scheduling a speaking engagement, or for information on any other books or teaching materials by Sara Berry, email us at info@bethelroadpublications.com.

Stones from the River Jordan is also available in an 8-Week Bible Study Audio Series taught by Sara Berry. A study guide accompanies the series. This *Stones from the River Jordan Study Guide* is also available separately for personal reflection while reading the book.

Sara's newest book, *Beyond Bethel*, is set to be released in 2011.

Check out our website for these and other materials.

www.bethelroadpublications.com

Tricia J. Robbins

Tricia Robbins resides in North Mississippi with her husband of 17 years, Shane, and two children she adores, Morgan and Ethan. Tricia currently works as the Client Advocate Director at Parkgate Pregnancy Clinic. She meets with teenage girls and women who find themselves in unplanned pregnancies, many who seek abortions.

Tricia counsels with these women to help them make life affirming decisions as she shares the Gospel with each one. Since childhood, Tricia has enjoyed a love for music as a violinist and pianist, teaching private music lessons for over 14 years. She also enjoys running and spending time with her precious family. She currently attends The Church at Trace Crossing and has been active in churches throughout adulthood, working in various ministries with children, inner-city youth, students, and adults. Serving Christ, her family, and hurting women is Tricia's deepest call. After being married to Shane for 17 years, she respects and loves him more than ever before. She talks to Hilarie every single day and they spend as much time together as possible, enjoying a love and unique relationship that only God could have created.

If you are interested in scheduling a speaking engagement, email us at info@bethelroadpublications.com.

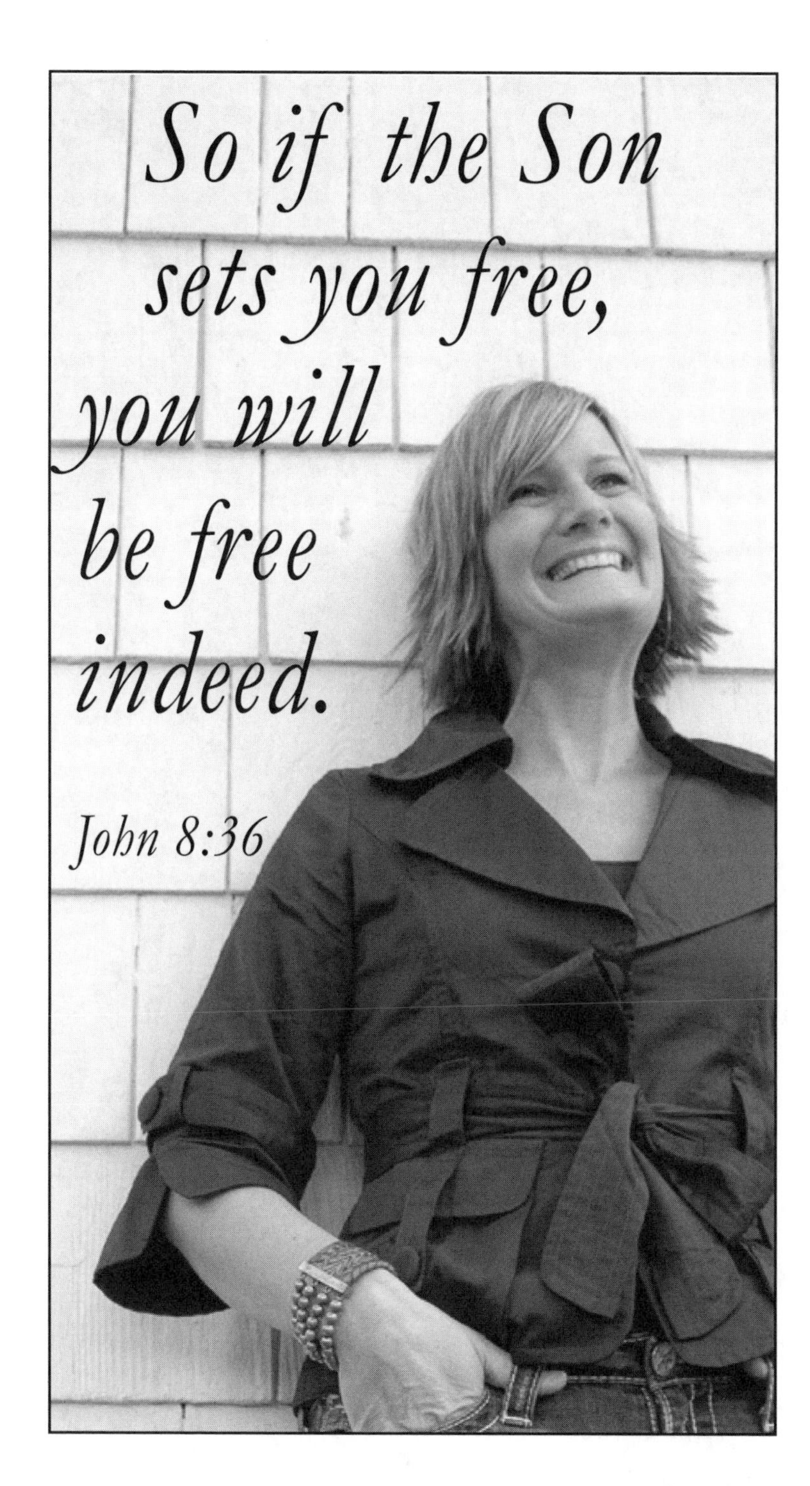
So if the Son
sets you free,
you will
be free
indeed.
John 8:36